# ANNE BRONTË

## The Other One

# Women Writers

General Editors: *Eva Figes* and *Adele King*

**Published titles:**

*Sylvia Plath:* Susan Bassnett
*Fanny Burney:* Judy Simons
*Christina Stead:* Diana Brydon
*Charlotte Brontë:* Pauline Nestor
*Margaret Atwood:* Barbara Hill Rigney
*Eudora Welty:* Louise Westling
*Anne Brontë:* Elizabeth Langland

**Forthcoming:**

*Jane Austen:* Meenakshi Mukherjee
*Elizabeth Barrett Browning:* Majorie Stone
*Elizabeth Bowen:* Phyllis Lassner
*Emily Brontë:* Lyn Pykett
*Ivy Compton Burnett:* Kathy Gentile
*Willa Cather:* Susie Thomas
*Colette:* Diana Holmes
*Emily Dickinson:* Joan Kirkby
*George Eliot:* Kristin Brady
*Mrs Gaskell:* Jane Spencer
*Doris Lessing:* Barbara Hill Rigney
*Katherine Mansfield:* Diane DeBell
*Christina Rossetti:* Linda Marshall
*Jean Rhys:* Carol Rumens
*Stevie Smith:* Catherine Civello
*Muriel Spark:* Judith Sproxton
*Edith Wharton:* Katherine Joslin-Jeske
*Women in Romanticism:* Meena Alexander
*Virginia Woolf:* Clare Hanson

**Further titles are in preparation**

# Women Writers

# Anne Brontë
# The Other One

## Elizabeth Langland

MACMILLAN

© Elizabeth Langland 1989

All rights reserved. No reproduction, copy or transmission
of this publication may be made without written permission.

No paragraph of this publication may be reproduced, copied
or transmitted save with written permission or in accordance
with the provisions of the Copyright Act 1956 (as amended),
or under the terms of any licence permitting limited copying
issued by the Copyright Licensing Agency, 33-4 Alfred Place,
London WC1E 7DP.

Any person who does any unauthorised act in relation to
this publication may be liable to criminal prosecution and
civil claims for damages.

First published 1989

Published by
MACMILLAN EDUCATION LTD
Houndmills, Basingstoke, Hampshire RG21 2XS
and London
Companies and representatives
throughout the world

Printed in the People's Republic of China

British Library Cataloguing in Publication Data
Langland, Elizabeth
    Anne Brontë: the other one. — (Women
    writers).
    1. Fiction in English. Brontë, Anne, 1820–
    1849. Critical studies
    I. Title    II. Series
    823'.8

ISBN 0-333-42300-3
ISBN 0-333-42301-1 Pbk

# Contents

*To Deirdre and Edith Crossland*
*who first introduced me*
*to Yorkshire and Brontë country.*

# Acknowledgements

I am grateful to my friends of long-standing in Yorkshire who have shared and fostered my love of the Brontës for many years. I am particularly grateful to Edith Crossland for taking the time to drive me to Brontë houses, schools, and locales and to Deirdre Crossland for hosting me and organising a trip to Scarborough to visit the sea and Anne's grave.

I thank the University of Florida for grants enabling me to pursue research in England and Juliet R. V. Barker, Librarian/Curator of the Brontë Parsonage Museum, for facilitating that research. I appreciate my students in Victorian literature for sharing my enthusiasm for Anne Brontë; my parents, Joseph and Judith Langland, for encouraging this project; and my children, Erika and Peter, for listening with interest to countless Brontë anecdotes. To my colleague, Alistair Duckworth, I owe a debt of gratitude for his careful reading of the final manuscript. And for cheerfully reading draft upon draft, I thank my husband, Jerald Jahn, whose constant support made my task even pleasant.

# Editors' Preface

The study of women's writing has been long neglected by a male critical establishment both in academic circles and beyond. As a result, many women writers have either been unfairly neglected or have been marginalised in some way, so that their true influence and importance has been ignored. Other women writers have been accepted by male critics and academics, but on terms which seem, to many women readers of this generation, to be false or simplistic. In the past the internal conflicts involved in being a woman in a male-dominated society have been largely ignored by readers of both sexes, and this has affected our reading of women's work. The time has come for a serious reassessment of women's writing in the light of what we understand today.

This series is designed to help in that reassessment.

All the books are written by women because we believe that men's understanding of feminist critique is only, at best, partial. And besides, men have held the floor quite long enough.

EVA FIGES
ADELE KING

# 1 Anne Brontë's Life: 'age and experience'

Just as it has been inevitable that Anne Brontë should be seen within the context of her more famous sisters, Emily and Charlotte, so it has been inevitable that she has been done the least justice in that context. We must see her in that context to understand her, but we must also recognise the ways in which she casts her own lights and is not merely a reflection of her greater sisters. Anne's personality, interests, and experiences all shaped for her an increasingly individual approach to life, an approach necessarily reflected in her art. But, too often, rather than receive recognition for its distinction, Anne's literary achievement has been perceived as a colourless shadow of her sisters'.

Anne's position as the youngest in the family – the 'baby' – surely accounts for part of what has been her reputation. It is generally agreed that, however solicitous Charlotte may have been of Anne's health, she was often deprecatory of her talents. And it was Charlotte who early set the tone for evaluating Anne. While we should not underestimate the service Charlotte performed in galvanising her two younger sisters into print, we should note that once they were in print Charlotte seemed incapable of appreciating Anne's unique gifts as poet and novelist.

Previous studies of the Brontës have tended to focus on the close working relationship the sisters shared, a literary bond forged in childhood through the mythical worlds they jointly created. Less attention has been paid to the tensions and divergent interests among the three famous women, but it is here we must now focus because it is obvious that three people of such talent, even genius, and of increasingly divergent experiences as they achieved maturity would necessarily produce very different kinds of novels, often to the distaste of one another.

The differences, of course, were not borne simply of post-childhood experiences. It is increasingly evident that the early loss of a mother and two sisters and the unique isolation of the maturing girls and their brother, Branwell, generated sharply different roles for each even as they conduced to a peculiarly intense intimacy.

In Anne, these conditions generated a strong sense of guilt with which she grappled emotionally and intellectually throughout her life. They created an equally strong sense of responsibility and a tenacious determination to become independent and successful outside the home. And, in sharp contrast to their effects on her sisters, these conditions produced in Anne a lively distrust of romantic posturings and a predilection for a clear-sighted realism.

I

Anne was born in Thornton, on January 17, 1820, three months prior to her family's removal to the parsonage at Haworth upon Mr Brontë's appointment to the 'perpetual curacy' there. Shortly after the move, Mrs Brontë was diagnosed as having cancer (although recent research suggests her illness may have been the cumulative result of too frequent childbearing[1]) and was confined in pain to her bedroom until her death on September 21, 1821, when Anne was only twenty months old. It is impossible at this distance to calculate the effects of that serious illness and death upon the infant daughter who would have no 'memory' of her mother, but, when we consider that psychologists believe that the personality is largely formed by eighteen months, we must suspect a deep influence. It is perhaps in these events that we find the root of Anne's crushing sense of sin and her preoccupation with the doctrines of 'Election' and 'Reprobation', doctrines espousing foreordained salvation or damnation. She of all her siblings seemed to feel it most necessary to square her experience in the world with a divine plan. She, of them all, seemed most afflicted by a sense of her personal unworthiness. Winifred Gérin, in her biography of Anne Brontë, has laid the responsibility for this early disposition at the door of Miss Branwell, the mother's elder sister, who ultimately replaced the mother in fact if not in spirit within the parsonage.[2] But this interpretation does not comfortably accord with Miss Branwell's own membership in the Wesleyan branch of Methodism which preached 'Redemption for All' in opposition to that of the Calvinist Methodists who prophesied redemption only for the 'Elect'. Growing up in a minister's household, the children would all be aware of these sharp debates; more significant, Anne had just been born when her mother, the natural stable point of her world and focus of her developing personality, was removed by illness and death. That loss alone could account for her personal insecurity and doubt, for her preoccupation with life after death, for a sense of guilt and responsibility. It is also a pattern that would have been etched still more deeply by the early death of her oldest sister and surrogate mother, Maria, when Anne was only five.

Anne's autobiographical poem, 'Self-Communion', lends support for this interpretation of the shaping forces of her young personality. There, her account of her childhood emphasises 'a helpless child,/Feeble and full of causeless fears,/ . . . finding in protecting love/Its only refuge

from despair'. She recognises the contextual basis for her
feelings of helplessness, describing a world 'where truth
maintains so little sway,/Where seeming fruit is bitter
dust,/And kisses oft to death betray'.[3]

One anecdote survives from Anne's infancy, and, ironically, that anecdote speaks to Anne's religious disposition.
We must wonder if it was embellished by time and further
shaped by the personalities that ultimately emerged. Nancy
Garrs, the children's nursemaid, 'who lived to a great
old age, used to recall how "when Anne was a baby,
Charlotte rushed into her Papa's study to say that there
was an angel standing by Anne's cradle, but when they
returned it was gone, though Charlotte was sure she had
seen it"'.[4] The episode certainly speaks to Charlotte's
estimate of Anne as one destined for heaven.

Anne, from childhood on, was the most obviously delicate
of the Brontë children. She suffered from asthma and was
an easy prey to colds and influenza. This weakness caused
Charlotte to recall later in life that Anne, since 'early childhood . . . seemed preparing for an early death'.[5] Judgments
of Anne's physical infirmity seem to have led Charlotte
unconsciously to corollary judgments of relative weakness
of character and intellect. But Anne was, of the sisters,
perhaps the most rigorously logical, the most quietly obser-
vant, the most realistic, and, in certain spheres, the most
tenacious, the most determined, and the most courageous.
All of these qualities were to emerge as her life unfolded.

In the famous story of the 'Masks', reported by Elizabeth
Gaskell in her *Life of Charlotte Brontë*, Anne gives evidence
of her character and mind. Mr Brontë reported to Mrs
Gaskell that 'When my children were very young . . . the
youngest [Anne] about four, thinking that they knew more
than I had yet discovered, in order to make them speak
with less timidity, I deemed that if they were put under
a sort of cover I might gain my end; and happening to
have a mask in the house, I told them all to stand and

speak boldly from under the cover of the mask'.[6] It is a charming story because the mask could hardly provide any genuine cover, yet the children's responses to the questions they were put are telling. Anne was asked 'what a child like her most wanted; she answered, "Age and experience"'. Very few papers or letters written by Anne survived her death, yet in one of the few to remain – Anne Brontë's Birthday Note, July 30, 1841 – Anne at twenty-one queries, 'What will the next four years bring forth? Providence only knows. But we ourselves have sustained very little alteration since that time. I have the same faults that I had then, only I have more wisdom and experience, and a little more self-possession than I then enjoyed' (LL 1 239). It seems that the child of four was indeed the mother of the woman. Anne still valued experience and the wisdom and self-possession her years had brought.

Anne penned this letter while serving as governess at Thorp Green, and that context allows us to recognise that, for Anne, 'wisdom and experience' meant wisdom and experience of the larger social world, a wisdom and experience that would ultimately feed her religious meditations and her artistic production and would ultimately culminate in a final wish to leave the moors at Haworth and return to the sea at Scarborough to be buried.

## II

We need to trace the steps that led to Anne's independent spirit and election of difference. 1824 was a year that saw many changes in Anne's life as she had known it to that point. In the spring, Miss Branwell, the mother's sister and the children's aunt, took up permanent residence at Haworth parsonage as surrogate mother. Her more stern disposition made it impossible that she could ever replace the mother, but she did take responsibility for certain domestic decisions. Apparently it was, at least in part, due to Miss Branwell's unwillingness to undertake the education of her nieces that Maria and Elizabeth were enrolled at Cowan Bridge School on July 1; Charlotte followed on August 10, and Emily joined them on November 25. Anne was left at home with Branwell, whose education Mr Brontë was superintending. One lasting benefit of this scheme to Anne was her acquisition of Latin, apparent evidence that Anne joined Branwell (then and thereafter) in his studies. In any case, she achieved a greater mastery of Latin than either of her sisters.[7] Although only four and a half, Anne was also in a position to witness Branwell's attempt to attend Haworth Grammar School.[8] It was a failure, as so many of his ventures were later to be, and it is not unreasonable to think that Anne was already developing the maturity to perceive the failure and to contemplate the underlying causes. The different education given to boys and girls and its disastrous consequences to both sexes are subjects which she addresses eloquently in *The Tenant of Wildfell Hall*. The protagonist, Helen Graham, is particularly adamant about the harmful effects of boy's education, founded on principles at once narrow and promiscuous. I quote at length because it is a substantial statement, one that perhaps stems from Anne's experiences of Branwell:

Well then, it must be that you think they [boys and girls] are *both* weak and prone to err, and the slightest error, the merest shadow of pollution, will ruin the one, while the character of the other will be strengthened and embellished – his education properly finished by a little practical acquaintance with forbidden things. Such experience, to him, (to use a trite simile), will be like the storm to the oak, which, though it may scatter the leaves, and snap the smaller branches, serves but to rivet the roots, and to harden and condense the fibres of the tree. You would have us encourage our sons to prove all things by their own experience, while our daughters must not even profit by the experience of others. Now *I* would have both so to benefit by the experience of others, and the precepts of higher authority, that they should know beforehand to refuse the evil and choose the good, and require no experimental proofs to teach them the evil of transgression. I would not send a poor girl into the world unarmed against her foes, and ignorant of the snares that beset her path . . . and as for my son – if I thought he would grow up to be what you call a man of the world – one that has *seen life* . . . . – I would rather that he died to-morrow![9]

These sentiments are radical for Anne Brontë's day, and she recognised they would be met with hostility, a hostility that she allows a vicar in the novel to voice as he characterises Helen Graham's views as 'criminal . . . making a fool of the boy' (TWH 64). But Anne had the example of Branwell for her justification.

There is little evidence of rapport between the brother and youngest sister, and it may have been that Branwell was sensitive enough to feel his little sister's silent judgment and condemnation. This reading of affairs would help to explain his contemptuous dismissal of Anne in 1834: Anne is 'nothing, absolutely nothing . . . next door to an idiot'.[10] Although a brotherly arrogance leads him also to unflattering views of Emily ('lean and scant, with a face about the size of a penny') and Charlotte ('a broad dumpy thing'), with them he confines himself to physical appearances. With Anne, the condemnation is broader.

In any case, Anne and Branwell were not to continue alone for long. On February 14, 1825 Maria arrived home from Cowan Bridge seriously ill. She died on May 6 of that year, an event shortly followed by Elizabeth's May 31 departure from Cowan Bridge with Charlotte and

Emily. Elizabeth, also ill, shared her older sister's fate and died on June 15. Charlotte was to immortalise this school and her experience of its abuses that precipitated her sisters' deaths as 'Lowood' in *Jane Eyre*.

These two sudden and unexpected deaths had a dramatic impact on the remaining children, particularly the death of Maria who had served as mother to them all. Charlotte was now the eldest and on her naturally devolved a sense of responsibility for the younger children. But Charlotte appears not to have shared Maria's maternal nature, and she was to struggle with and, at times, to resent the burden and responsibilities she had inherited (LL I 82-83).

The debacle of Cowan Bridge determined Mr Brontë to educate his remaining children at home, and, for the next five and a half years, they remained at the parsonage, developing their extraordinary minds in part through the creation of fantasy worlds: Angria and Gondal. Angria owes its creation to the gift to Branwell of a set of toy soldiers which Mr Brontë purchased at Leeds on June 5, 1826. Each of the sisters and the brother immediately seized upon one as a personal favourite: Charlotte describes the incident:

> . . . next morning Branwell came to our door with a box of soldiers. Emily and I jumped out of bed, and I snatched up one and exclaimed: 'This is the Duke of Wellington! This shall be the Duke!' When I had said this Emily likewise took one up and said it should be hers; when Anne came down, she said one should be hers. Mine was the prettiest of the whole, and the tallest, and the most perfect in every part. Emily's was a grave-looking fellow, and we called him 'Gravey'. Anne's was a queer little thing, much like herself, and we called him 'Waiting-boy'. Branwell chose his, and called him Buonaparte.[11]

For four and a half years the children collaborated in the creation of a mythical kingdom of Angria, generating a literature, a history, a politics. But Angria seems always to have been more of Charlotte's and Branwell's inspiration, and Anne and Emily began to draw away to create their own, more feminine world, Gondal. This detachment was hastened by Charlotte's departure for boarding school in January 1831 and Branwell's increasing control and imposition of his interests in military campaigns.

The four children had, essentially, paired up. Charlotte had become Branwell's boon companion, and Emily and Anne had forged a relationship so close that Charlotte's school friend, Ellen Nussey, would shortly describe them as 'twins'.

The major influence in Anne's childhood and adolescence was her sister Emily. When Emily returned from Cowan Bridge, the proximity in ages made the two sisters natural companions. To this nearness in ages was added a shared delight in roaming over the neighbouring countryside. With Emily, Anne discovered a joyous natural world, and her keen delight in that world is recorded in her earliest poems. In a poem from her sixteenth year, Anne writes:

For long ago I love to lie
    Upon the pathless moor,
To hear the wild wind rushing by
    With never ceasing roar;

Its sound was music then to me;
    Its wild and lofty voice
Made by [sic] heart beat exultingly
    And my whole soul rejoice (P 49).

Later, away from Haworth, Anne would recall the joy in nature that she associates with a deep sense of kinship in the world, conferred by Emily's presence and the intense intimacy they shared.

There is a silent eloquence
In every wild bluebell
That fills my softened heart with bliss
That words could never tell.

Those sunny days of merriment
When heart and soul were free,
And when I dwelt with kindred hearts
That loved and cared for me (P 73–74).

And, at subsequent later periods, even when depressed by loneliness, privation, and difficulty, Anne was still able to recapture the rapture that immersion in the natural world could generate in her.

Emily's influence cannot be underestimated during this period of Anne's youth. The earliest protrait of the two that we have from an outsider, the words of Ellen Nussey in July of 1833, emphasises their remarkable bond. Because these observations are some of the very few we have of the two youngest Brontës, they are worth quoting at length:

Emily had by this time acquired a lithesome, graceful figure. She was the tallest person in the house, except her father. Her hair, which was naturally as beautiful as Charlotte's, was in the same unbecoming tight curl and frizz, and there was the same want of complexion. She had very beautiful eyes – kind, kindling, liquid eyes; but she did not often look at you: she was too reserved. Their colour might be said to be dark grey, at other times dark blue, they varied so. She talked very little. She and Anne were like twins – inseparable companions, and in the very closest sympathy, which never had any interruption.

Anne, dear, gentle Anne, was quite different in appearance from the others. She was her aunt's favourite. Her hair was a very pretty, light brown, and fell on her neck in graceful curls. She had lovely violet-blue eyes, fine pencilled eyebrows, and clear, almost transparent complexion (LL I 112).

In addition to the statement that Emily and Anne were 'like twins', we also learn that Anne had a superior complexion and hair to her -sisters', confirmation that she was the pretty one of the Brontës. She was also clearly her aunt's favourite. These two facts may help account for the confidence expressed in her greater willingness to seek a life for herself outside the parsonage.

Consequently, when Charlotte was offered a post at Roe Head School in the summer of 1835, it was Anne who ultimately benefited from the offer of free schooling for a sister. Emily, as the elder, naturally was chosen to go first and left with Charlotte on July 29. But by mid October, Charlotte had obtained Emily's recall, believing she would otherwise perish from homesickness. Sometime before October 27, Anne was sent to Roe Head to replace Emily.

Anne too suffered intensely at school, both emotionally and physically; yet, in her determination not to give up, we see the first convincing evidence of her real difference from Emily in both character and disposition. Emily was physically strong, courageous, spirited, and independent. But she would not do what Anne would, that is, submit herself to alien discipline. Anne had formed a resolution to learn as much as she could with the idea of ultimately supporting herself. Whereas Charlotte seems to have accepted the *necessity* of this course, Anne, in contrast, seems to have accepted it as both necessary and *desirable*. Perhaps, the difference originated in Anne's greater distance from Branwell, in age and disposition. I have suggested earlier that she was soon aware of the failures of his education in the light of his character. In witnessing his lapses, Anne may have discovered within herself a desire to be free of such crippling dependencies. Her quiet observation of Branwell and her rigorous logic

would have instructed her in the benefits of acquiring
tools that would enable her to be self-determining.

Certain it is that Anne submitted herself to the discipline
of Roe Head School, winning a conduct prize at the end of
her first year.[12] What made Anne's task yet more difficult,
however, was the distance that existed between Charlotte
and her. Charlotte was going through her own crisis, feeling
revulsion at the prospect of endless teaching, a profession
for which she felt no calling. There is no evidence that Anne
and Charlotte had ever been particularly close emotionally,
and it may be that Charlotte looked on her youngest
sister with some resentment. After all, it was her felt
obligation to help with her sisters' education that kept
Charlotte trapped at Roe Head School. And, Charlotte
was determined not to show her youngest sister any special
favours, so she may have adopted even more distance than
was necessary (LL I 136–164).

A recognition of distance between the two young sisters
is a necessary corrective, one that allows us to discount
much of Charlotte's judgment of Anne's literary work.
Although bound by common goals, common ties, and
a common past, the sisters were temperamentally very
different. The older sister, emotional and romantic, chaffed
at her lot; the younger one grew increasingly logical
and practical, determined to wrest success from her pain.

At Roe Head Charlotte's disposition and her preoccupations blinded her to Anne's suffering and worsening
health. Anne had become gravely ill before Charlotte
recognised any symptoms, and then Charlotte's sense of
guilt and remorse was so great that she turned on Miss
Wooler (the director of Roe Head), blaming her for
Anne's condition (LL I 163–64).

When, exactly, Anne became ill and whether she suffered
one illness or two during 1837 are questions impossible to
resolve without further evidence.[13] More important is the
religious crisis that accompanied her bodily collapse. No

doubt, the spiritual and physical crises intensified each other. At this low ebb, Anne Brontë 'urgently requested' a visit from the minister of the Moravian church at Mirfield, Reverend James La Trobe. An understanding of the differences between the Moravians and the Methodists may explain Anne's state of mind and unusual request. The Moravian religion focused on pardon and peace; it recognised the possibility of doubt and failure even in the redeemed, and Anne may have needed this assurance in her dark day. Reverend La Trobe, who wrote an account of this meeting, commented: 'her life hung on a slender thread. She soon got over the shyness natural on seeing a perfect stranger. The words of love, from Jesus, opened her heart to my words, and she was very grateful for my visits. I found her well acquainted with the main truths of the Bible respecting our salvation, *but seeing them more through the law than the Gospel, more as a requirement from God than His Gift in His Son*, but her heart opened to the sweet views of salvation, pardon and peace in the blood of Christ'.[14]

Anne survived this crisis, but its character was already marking preoccupations in her very different from those of her siblings. Much of her poetry after this period deals with religious themes, and it constitutes a moving spiritual autobiography. *The Tenant of Wildfell Hall* also develops the themes of election, reprobation, and salvation that were becoming so near to Anne Brontë's heart.

Anne spent 1838 at home, having completed two and a quarter years at Roe Head. Her education was sufficient to equip her for a position as governess, and with quiet determination she pursued her goal of independence and competency.

While Anne was at home in 1838, Emily was away for at least six months at Law Hill, Halifax in a teaching position that Charlotte characterised as 'slavery' (LL I 162). When Emily returned home, unable to continue, Anne felt it her duty to take up employment. For Anne, perhaps it

was more than duty, more a prompting to be on her own
and contributing to the family. She left Haworth on April
8, 1839 to assume a post at Blake Hall as governess for the
Ingham family, of whose five children Anne would have the
care of only the eldest two, a boy of six and a girl of five.
Many of Anne's experiences at Blake Hall no doubt make
up the material of her first novel, *Agnes Grey*, although it
is simplistic to assume the fictional world merely replicated
life. The novel offers us, however, some glimpses of why
this first position was to prove disastrous for Anne. We
are given portraits of unruly children, entirely without
discipline, given to cruelty and maliciousness. They were
a species totally alien to their eighteen-year-old governess,
who found them unmanageable, and this first venture culminated in Anne's dismissal at the end of the year (LL I 196).

Anne's spirit, however, was undaunted, and it may have
been as early as May of 1840 that she assumed her second
position, this time as governess for the Robinsons at Thorp
Green (P 10–11). Anne's spirit is remarkable perhaps only
in view of Charlotte's estimation of her youngest sister.
Charlotte wrote to Ellen Nussey on Anne's departure for
Blake Hall: 'Poor child! She left us last Monday no one
went with her – it was her own wish that she might be
allowed to go alone – as she thought she could manage better
and summon more courage if thrown entirely upon her own
resources' (LL I 175). In Anne's determination we should
recognise the resolve of the four-year-old speaking from
behind the mask who wanted only 'age and experience'.
Charlotte continues: 'You would be astonished what a
sensible, clever letter she writes . . .' and so unconsciously
betrays her estimate of Anne and Anne's competence.

Before assuming her post at Thorp Green, Anne was at
home for at least four months, and it appears that during this
time Anne became acquainted with her father's new curate,
William Weightman. He had taken up duties at Haworth
Church on August 19, 1839, and had brought joy and delight

to all the inhabitants of the parsonage through his good nature and lively manner. Recent criticism of Anne Brontë has pointed to William Weightman as a significant love and loss in Anne's life. Whether Anne held her father's curate in any special regard – indeed, loved him – remains unclear; Charlotte's letters to Ellen Nussey are full of details of his flirtations and of the various new conquests he has made. At first, Anne is not mentioned. It is only recent research that has allowed us to piece together a picture of Anne's affection for Weightman. The only contemporaneous reference to such a possibility comes in Charlotte's letter of January 20, 1842 to Ellen Nussey. Charlotte comments:

> Your darling 'his young reverence' as you tenderly call him – is looking delicate and pale – poor thing, don't you pity him? I do, from my heart – when he is well and fat and jovial I never think of him – but when anything ails him I am always sorry – He sits opposite to Anne at church sighing softly and looking out of the corners of his eyes to win her attention – and Anne is so quiet, her look so downcast – they are a picture (LL I 250).

Critics have sought evidence for a growing love and understanding between Anne and William in a number of 'love' poems that make up Anne's poetic corpus. There, a man with features like Weightman's ('sunny smile', 'light heart') plays a significant part until an untimely death, like Weightman's. But the seven poems out of which this argument is constructed are not clearly referring to Weightman; two, indeed, appear in the two novels, *Agnes Grey* and *The Tenant of Wildfell Hall* and their dates of composition are uncertain. They could reasonably refer only to the fictional situations in the novels. Also, other of the supposed love poems are arguably Gondal in origin.[15]

Finally, other evidence points to Anne's merely sisterly affection for the man who helped her with Branwell through some difficult episodes. First, if she loved Weightman, it

is difficult to explain why she returned to Thorp Green in
January 1842 when the departure of Emily and Charlotte
for Brussels made it the logical course for Anne to return
to Haworth to care for her father and gave her a perfect
excuse to be near Weightman. Second, Anne's poem 'The
Captive Dove', written mostly in the spring of 1842, closes
with lines devoid of any hope for a loving relationship:
'But thou, poor solitary dove,/Must make unheard thy
joyless moan;/The heart that nature formed to love/Must
pine neglected and alone' (P 93). Finally, in *The Tenant
of Wildfell Hall,* Anne seems to offer a parody of the
kind of church flirtations Charlotte's letter has described
and suggests that Anne would not approve Weightman's
'sighing softly and looking out of the corners of his eyes
to win her attention'. If '*they* are a picture', as Charlotte
notes, it may be because Anne is clearly disapproving as
does her character Helen Graham. When Helen's husband
confesses that 'for, all the two hours, I have been thinking
of you and wanting to catch your eyes, and you were so
absorbed in your devotions that you had not even a glance
to spare for me – I declare it is enough to make one
jealous of one's Maker', she chastises him for presuming
'to dispute possession of my heart with Him' (TWH 217).

Without further evidence we cannot know what the full
relationship was between Anne and Weightman. But we
can be sure that when he died quite suddenly in September
of 1842 the affection between them was sufficiently strong
that she experienced a deep sense of loss.

Anne held her position at Thorp Green for five years,
and for the rest of her life remained the valued friend
of the Robinson girls. The conditions that led to Anne's
decision to quit Thorp Green have unfortunately prevented
our learning first-hand information about her stay there.
Those conditions were caused by Branwell.

Anne was so successful as governess that, when the family
decided it was time to locate a tutor for their son, Anne

was able successfully to recommend Branwell. Branwell
had had difficulty securing posts or holding any of those
he did secure. Anne must have had some reservations about
Branwell's reliability; we can only speculate on why she
decided to recommend him. No doubt his company would
have been very welcome to her. A governess was neither fish
nor fowl – neither of the servant class nor of the upper classes she served. Her position was very lonely, and Branwell,
occupying a similar post, could have kept her company in
the hours when she was free from her duties. Also, Anne
may have felt that her presence would be an encouraging and
stabilising one for her brother. She perhaps further believed
that she could redeem him from his evil propensities.

Branwell joined Anne when she returned to Thorp Green
in January 1843, after the Christmas holidays. For a time
the two prospered and were so well valued by the Robinson
family that Mr Brontë was invited to visit Thorp Green in
April of 1843. Anne was thoroughly engaged in her duties
and during 1843 and 1844 purchased a variety of teaching
materials, which indicate the commitment she felt to her
charges and her growing competence to instruct them.

But at some point in 1844, Branwell developed a passion
for Mrs Robinson which he believed she reciprocated. His
behaviour became so flagrant that eventually everyone in
the household became aware of it. In midsummer 1845,
Anne would note in her diary paper: 'During my stay
[at Thorp Green] I have had some very unpleasant and
undreamt-of experience of human nature . . .' (LL II 52).
And pencilled in the back of her prayer book are the words
'Sick of mankind and their disgusting ways.'[16] Her trouble
is vividly expressed in these words, yet she struggled on for
another year, hoping, it may be, still to rescue Branwell.
Anne has painted in *The Tenant of Wildfell Hall* just such
a picture of a woman idealistically bent on recovering
a man from vicious habits and sensual tendencies. Her
own emotions may have fed the picture and the ultimate

recognition of futility. Because fail she did. Anne gave
notice of her intention to quit the family in June of 1845.
Branwell stayed on, only to be dismissed in July when Mr
Robinson finally discovered his liaison with Mrs Robinson.

Branwell returned home, wild and distraught. He was
convinced that Mrs Robinson was only waiting for the
death of her husband, who was not expected to survive
long, before summoning him to her side for life. But when
her husband did die on May 26, 1846, Mrs Robinson made
it plain that she wished Branwell to keep his distance. The
Brontë family felt that Branwell had been the victim of
a worldly and designing woman, who clearly must have
encouraged Branwell to some extent, and, as future events
have demonstrated, never contemplated a serious liaison
with her children's tutor. Indeed, after a suitable period
of mourning, Mrs Robinson married an eligible widower.

No doubt the truth lies somewhere in between. Branwell
was entranced with the romance of marrying a lady;
and securing her wealth must have seemed an attractive
alternative to working in the menial posts he had held. One
unfortunate consequence of Branwell's dreams and disap-
pointments, however, was an hostility between the Brontës
and the Robinsons, an hostility aggravated by Mrs Gaskell's
biography of Charlotte which alienated the Robinson girls
and thus prevented them from volunteering crucial information about Anne during her Thorp Green years.

Meanwhile, Branwell's sense of loss and disappointment
was so keen that for the rest of his life he destroyed any
peace that might have subsisted in the parsonage. Alcohol
and opium ultimately killed him. Before that time, Emily
and Anne were responsible for getting him to bed after
his drinking bouts, for rescuing him from fire when
he ignited his sheets by smoking in bed. For a while,
Charlotte struggled to redeem Branwell, but she became
so disgusted that she ultimately ended all commerce with
her brother (LL II 64–66, 74, 76–77). She, of course,

was witnessing the absolute collapse of her childhood intimate.

During these seemingly inauspicious times, the three sisters began their publishing careers. For a long time, they had nurtured a dream of one day being able to open a school of their own at the parsonage. To that end, Emily and Charlotte had gone to Brussels in February of 1842 to master foreign languages. Charlotte had formed the scheme, and she had also selected Emily to accompany her although many considerations should have suggested Anne as the more suitable companion. Emily preferred to be at home; she would waste away in other environments. She was also much stronger physically than Anne and therefore better able to carry out the onerous tasks of washing, baking, and ironing of the parsonage. And the initial plan stipulated that one girl *should* stay at home to help Miss Branwell and to care for Mr Brontë. Apparently Charlotte felt she had to justify her procedure to Emily because she wrote on November 7: 'Anne seems omitted in the present plan but if all goes right I trust she will derive her full share of benefit from it in the end. I exhort all to hope . . .' (LL I 247). But, as I noted earlier, rather than stay at home, Anne resolutely determined that she would return to Thorp Green. Even her aunt's death in November, which returned Emily permanently to the parsonage and provided each girl with a legacy, failed to alter Anne's determination to continue working away from home. Two suggestive conclusions emerge from this sequence of events: first, that Anne and Charlotte were not close, and their interests and temperaments were increasingly differing, and second, that Emily and Anne, once so intimate, were now pursuing clearly divergent paths. Increasingly, Anne was to chart her own course and, with the distance conferred by age and experience, to become herself a critical judge of the 'twin' with whom she had once shared and empathised.

Charlotte's plans of qualifying themselves to open a
school were coming to fruition at the very moment that
Branwell was beginning his decline, and his perpetual
drunkenness effectually destroyed their dream although it
already seemed doomed by their failure to attract students.
At this time of near paralysis for the family, Charlotte
happened to discover some of Emily's poetry, a momentous
event which she described years later:

> One day in the autumn of 1845 I accidentally lighted
> on a MS. volume of verse in my sister Emily's hand-
> writing. Of course I was not surprised, knowing that
> she could and did write verse. I looked it over, and
> something more than surprise seized me – a deep
> conviction that there were not common effusions, nor
> at all like the poetry women generally write (LL II 79).

Charlotte's conviction of the poems' excellence led her to
urge publication on the reluctant Emily who was deeply
offended by Charlotte's violation of her privacy. Nonetheless, Charlotte prevailed, and Anne offered her own
poems to join those of Emily.

The sisters' first joint effort in authorship culminated
in a volume of poetry, *Poems, by Currer, Ellis, and Acton
Bell*, each girl preserving her initials in the pseudonym.
Charlotte explained the rationale of the pseudonyms, 'the
ambiguous choice being dictated by a sort of conscientious
scruple at assuming Christian names positively masculine,
while we did not like to declare ourselves women, because
. . . we had a vague impression that authoresses are liable
to be looked on with prejudice . . .' (LL II 70–80). The
volume was published in May 1846 by Messrs Aylott &
Jones of Paternoster Row, at the Brontë sisters' own cost,
fixed at £31 10s. The poems found a few favourable
reviewers but, by and large, passed unnoticed. Their

significance lay in opening up the world of publication to the sisters. Even before the poems appeared, as early as April 6, Charlotte was writing to publishers about fiction underway. Charlotte was working on *The Professor*, Emily on *Wuthering Heights*, and Anne on *Agnes Grey*.

In May 1847, in a surprising turn of events, Emily and Anne's novels were accepted and Charlotte's rejected by Thomas Newby. He asked the authors to share the risk of publication to the extent of £50 and, although the sisters had agreed not to lay out more of their precious legacy from their aunt in payment for publication, Anne and Emily jointly decided to meet his terms. Their act reveals how committed they were to publication and tends to dispel myths that publication and the attendant publicity were what Emily most sought to avoid. Charlotte pursued publication for *The Professor* and ultimately met with encouragement from Smith, Elder & Co. at Cornhill to submit another novel, if she had one. She had just finished *Jane Eyre*, shipped it off, had it instantly accepted and published by October 16, 1847, two months before Emily's and Anne's novels, languishing at Newby's, saw print.

Continually threatening this productivity was the presence of Branwell who worsened daily, making frequent demands upon the emotional and physical reserves of his sisters. Anne channelled many of her feelings and experiences into her second novel, *The Tenant of Wildfell Hall*. Writing was one way of coming to terms with the degradation he had introduced into their family circle.

Anne was, however, unfortunate in her publisher, Mr Newby, who proved to be unscrupulous in his efforts to maximise sales of the now popular Bells. *Jane Eyre* had met with brilliant success and Newby, hoping to capitalise on its popularity, billed *The Tenant* as by the same hand. This claim mortified both Anne and Charlotte; more seriously, it jeopardised Charlotte's position at Cornhill because she had promised them her next novel. On the spur of the moment on July 7, 1848, Anne and Charlotte resolved to hurry to London and, by confronting Smith, Elder & Co., convince them there were indeed three Bells. It seems a bold, perhaps uncharacteristic step, but it reveals the serious pride of authorship of each writer. It tells us more immediately and convincingly than any words could that Anne wished her art to be taken as hers and on its own terms.

*The Tenant of Wildfell Hall* was published in early July 1848. Throughout much of the spring of that year, Anne had been seriously ill, yet she persevered with her writing. The novel was an immediate and sensational success, only exceeded by Charlotte's success with *Jane Eyre*. On July 22 of the same year Anne was busy at work writing a preface to the second edition. In this important essay, she distinguishes her identity from those of Currer and Ellis Bell, obviously anxious and eager to establish her subjects and perspectives apart from theirs. In later chapters, we shall examine more fully the differences between Anne's work and her sisters'. Here, we may simply affirm the very different contexts and inclinations out of which the art grew.

Anne's faltering health and the crisis created by Branwell made further sustained efforts in fiction impossible. On September 24, 1848, Branwell died, ending his own misery and that of his long-suffering family. The cause of death was given as 'chronic bronchitis and marasmus'; in short, dissipation, not disease, killed him.[17] Emily caught cold at his funeral, refused all medical aid, and it was shortly clear that her life was in grave danger from consumption. To Charlotte belonged the agonised perception that neither Anne nor Emily was likely to last a year. Although Charlotte had been struggling to complete *Shirley*, all literary effort had to be suspended in face of the tragedy confronting her.

Emily died on December 19, allowing a doctor to be called only on that last day, when she was clearly beyond all help. In contrast, Anne struggled to live. A specialist, Dr Teale, was brought in to consult on her health on

January 5, 1849, but he could see that there was nothing to be done. Anne's moving final poem, begun two days after the doctor's visit, expresses simultaneous resignation to God's will and a fervent hope for miraculous recovery. There was no miracle, but there was great heroism. Anne faced her death with equanimity.

Her final wish was to revisit York Minster and the sea at Scarborough. In pursuit of this goal, she was indefatigable. Charlotte naturally worried that Anne's strength was unequal to the trip, but Anne was so determined that she enlisted Ellen Nussey in her plans. Ultimately, Anne, Charlotte, and Ellen set forth for Scarborough via York on May 24. Merely to be accomplishing her goal allowed Anne to rally momentarily. Once there, Anne had a sensation of regret that she had complicated things for Charlotte who would likely have to bury her away from Haworth. But Charlotte later wrote: 'I wanted her to die where she would be happiest. She loved Scarbro' (LL II 338). At the end, it was Anne who was exhorting Charlotte: 'Take courage, Charlotte, *take courage*'! (LL II 336).

Anne died on May 28, 1849, twenty-nine years of age. She is buried in St Mary's churchyard, Scarborough, the only one of the Brontës to be buried away from Haworth. This fact itself is an eloquent testimony to her individuality, which has too often been lost in myths of the Brontë sisters.

## III

The world in which Anne Brontë lived and wrote saw the beginnings of a longstanding Victorian debate on the Woman Question: what was woman's nature and what was her proper sphere? The urgency and pervasiveness of that debate is nowhere better revealed than in the lives of the Brontës, who, despite their seclusion, nonetheless wrote novels that spoke to its very heart.

By and large, Victorians believed woman belonged in
the home where she served as presiding angel. Although
the most famous representation of this notion – the Angel
in the House – did not appear until 1854–56 in Coventry
Patmore's poem of that name, the idea was gaining currency
from the beginning of the century. Briefly, the myth of
the angel in the house idealised woman and her innocence
in ways that made central her confinement to a separate
domestic sphere, where, free from the vicious influence
of the competitive business world, she could preserve
the nation's moral values. Even Victorians who did not
subscribe to the idea of the Angel in the House were
attracted to the implicit ideal of woman's redemptive
or salvatory potential. Victorian fiction is peopled with
a variety of idealistic, high-minded, and compassionate
heroines who embody values seen as distinctively feminine
in contrast to masculine aggressiveness and competitiveness.
The Victorian preoccupation with woman's special nature
developed into an ideology that legitimised unequal power
relations in the economic and political sphere even as it
glorified women's role in the domestic and 'moral' sphere.

Not surprisingly, then, the myth of the domestic heaven
often concealed the reality of a domestic hell. Women had
no legal status; they were non-persons under the law. A
woman stood in relationship to her husband as did her
children, entirely dependent on his will, responsibility, and
generosity. She could be abused physically and emotionally,
yet she was powerless to walk away. She had no rights over
her children. Her husband could squander his own fortune
as well as hers, seize any earnings that might accrue from her
efforts, yet she had no recourse. Under the law, her earnings
were his earnings. She could not sue for divorce under any
circumstances – the utmost divorce she could obtain was
permission to live alone – although, if she were proven
guilty of infidelity, he could divorce her. A full awareness
of these inequities in British law informs Anne Brontë's

novel *The Tenant of Wildfell Hall,* which also explodes the myth of domestic heaven and exposes the domestic hell, from which the protagonist ultimately flees into hiding.

Brontë recognised that this domestic heaven was jeopardised by the behaviour of women as well as that of men. She saw in her own pupils the effects of the narrow education prescribed for women. The goal of women's education in Victorian England was to provide little more than a finishing polish to a girl's manners by encouraging the acquisition of 'showy accomplishments . . . French, German, music, singing, dancing, fancy-work, and a little drawing'.[18] One powerless governess could do little to counteract the influence of a society bent on producing women whose minds were wholly occupied with details of costume, coquetry, and conquest. The lack of solid matter in these educational schemes created women ruled by vanity, vulnerable alike to their own weaknesses and to their parents' ambitions for their financially advantageous marriages.

It was almost impossible for a woman to secure a good education except by dint of self-application and discipline, yet there, too, she was inevitably limited. The universities were barred to her. Even a woman as distinguished as George Eliot was ambivalent about the effects of a rigorous course of education on woman's nature. The efforts by Barbara Bodichon and Emily Davies to establish a women's college in the 1860s met a chilly reception from men and women alike, although these determined women succeeded in founding Girton College in 1873. Women could not attend Oxford and Cambridge until the 1860s, and even then they could not earn degrees. Oxford did not admit its women students to full degrees and university membership until 1920; Cambridge delayed granting the same rights until 1948.[19]

Constrictions in educational opportunities were matched by the limited opportunities for employment afforded to women of the educated classes. Their options basically

resolved themselves down to two: educate other young
women and small children as a governess and schoolmistress
or become a writer. Anne Brontë's *Agnes Grey* presents
the difficulties of a young woman pursuing the first
option. Governessing usually entailed physical drudgery and
emotional battery. Unless a governess was very fortunate
in her family, she could expect to find that she would
be given entire responsibility for the children without
any significant power to exercise control. She stood in
an ambiguous social relationship to the family, neither
their equal nor clearly beneath them as were the other
servants. She experienced great loneliness and the frequent
humiliation of finding her often substantial talents ignored
or despised. Because opening one's own school freed one
from the social subjection of being a governess, many young
women strove to amass the resources to start their own
educational establishment. That, as we have seen, was the
Brontë sisters' plan until their own failure to gain pupils and
Branwell's worsening condition made the dream impossible.

The second 'profession' for women – writing – was
less socially acceptable. Charlotte Brontë early sought
encouragement to write poetry from Robert Southey and
was basically told that her business must be running
a household. Although she was discouraged, she was
not, fortunately, finally deterred. Yet women ventured
into print with caution and often, as did the Brontës,
employed male pseudonyms. That pseudonyms were widely
adopted by women speaks to two issues: first, their desire
to protect their privacy and to claim the wider subject
matter thought appropriate to male but not to female
writers; and second, a wish for a less prejudiced evaluation
of their works. Women writers were generally held in
mean estimation.

But even if women writers could be evaluated equally
with men and could lay claim to a comparable breadth of
social experience, they still found themselves constrained

and limited in the representation of their emotional experience. Victorian patriarchal ideology enforced views of good
women as essentially passionless. The representation of
female sexual passion, therefore, was largely taboo, a taboo
that still existed for Virginia Woolf in the early twentieth
century. In 'Professions for Women', Woolf claims that the
woman writer must·meet two challenges: first, killing the
Angel in the House, and second, telling the truth about her
own experiences as a being of flesh and blood. Although
she had met the first challenge, Woolf believed that no
woman had, as yet, successfully confronted the second.[20]

In the Victorian era, conceptions of a woman's sexuality
were tied to ideas of her moral nature and were most fully
articulated within the framework of the fallen woman and
the prostitute. The patriarchal ideology that professes to
explain the social event of a woman's fall has recourse
to woman's nature rather than her nurture. The fallen
woman, then, is a daughter of Eve, innately corrupt. This
ideological construction was so powerful that 'fallen' girls
of nine or ten (whom we would now recognise as innocent
victims of child abuse) could be comprehended within it.
And, although Victorians could distinguish among degrees
of fallen women, it rigidly maintained the moral chasm
that separated the fallen from the pure. The rise of
penitentiaries in the 1840s (homes of reclamation for fallen
women) stems from the belief in an innately corrupt female
nature because these penitentiaries emphasised a long
process requisite for spiritual purging and purification.

Looking back on the Victorian era, we find evidence that
many young women were victims of social circumstances.
They needed economic aid more than they needed moral
rescue. Their prostitution testified more to economic necessity and social vulnerability – a woman's powerless position
within patriarchy – than it did to moral perversion. Yet
the fear that morally corrupt tendencies in women might
suddenly mushroom into gigantic uncontrolled indulgences

was so pervasive that it received memorable representation in Charlotte Brontë's own madwoman in the attic, Bertha Mason in *Jane Eyre*, and it significantly constrained the legitimate representation of passion in women. Charlotte Brontë's representation of Bertha reveals the extent to which women writers, like men, were shaped by their culture's ideologies, and we must applaud the courage they found to begin exploring the depth of passion present in women. From these perspectives, we can more fully appreciate Anne Brontë's representation of Helen Graham Huntingdon, the runaway wife from *The Tenant of Wildfell Hall*. The creation of Helen, a woman 'fallen' by virtue of her flight, challenges a culture's myths of domestic happiness and the pure woman. Through Helen, Anne Brontë transforms our notions of both.

Anne Brontë lived and wrote at a time in history when women had gained some preliminary rights that enabled them to question their continuing disenfranchisement in other spheres. Brontë's novels constitute a significant contribution in the ongoing debate over laws, education and employment for women, and the ideology of womanhood. Her ability to write so forcefully and so directly about such sensitive subjects no doubt reflects the enabling sisterly context out of which her novels were born. That bond of common endeavour and affection, however, fuelled three *individual* talents and sharpened three *individual* perspectives, as we shall explore more fully in our examination of Anne's works.

# 2 Influences: 'Acton Bell is neither Currer nor Ellis Bell'

In the Brontë mythology of three talented, intimate and devoted sisters, Anne has played, in George Moore's words, the role of 'literary Cinderella', relegated to the ashes of history for her failure to reach the standards set by her sisters.[1] In short, it is usually assumed that Anne is trying to do what Emily and Charlotte are doing but that Anne cannot succeed through lack of talent. I suggest, instead, that Anne was self-consciously critiquing her sisters' work and establishing alternative standards and values. Ironically, Anne has played, *vis-a-vis* her sisters, the traditional role of the woman writer within patriarchy. That is, Anne is critiquing her sisters' works in the same way that women writers critique the values and standards of male writers. And rather than acknowledge the critique and distinction, we have measured the work by inappropriate standards which cannot do justice to its achievement. Such is often the fate of the woman writer in patriarchal culture. We might also note that as the surviving sister, Charlotte was in the position of 'patriarch' to determine which of Emily's and Anne's novels were reprinted and which were not.

Anne finally presents a very different feminism from Charlotte's and Emily's, one more influenced by the eighteenth century than by the Romantic poets and novelists who shaped her sisters. Anne's feminism focuses on the cultivation of reason and on nurture of the soul leading to conquest of the passions. Anne's heroines feel deeply but strive to discipline their passions. Charlotte and Emily, in contrast, define their heroines' strength in the force of their felt and represented passion, including, for Charlotte, sexual passion. Anne places personal independence and suitability of temperament with a man over sexual passion, and the consequences to her art are significant. In Anne's novels, heroines do not humble themselves before male aggression in the often disturbingly submissive manner of Charlotte's heroines. Anne shares with Emily a clear-eyed understanding of the cruelty to which passion coupled with power and mastery can lead. But Anne then departs from Emily in refusing to glorify that cruelty in a figure like Heathcliff. Anne rejects all glorification of male strength; her heroes are strong principally in moral conviction. And marriage for her heroines appears as a coda to the novel rather than as a condition of the protagonist's happiness. A study of the intertextual relationships among the Brontës poems and novels may thus bring Anne's achievement into the light.

Anne Brontë's poetry, ultimately less powerful than her novels, nonetheless constitutes a fine body of meditative and introspective verse. Although most of this poetry remains unknown, Anne did write several hymn-like poems which both fed on the evangelical hymn writing tradition and contributed to it. Edward Chitham, who has prepared the definitive edition of Anne's poetry, notes that three of her hymns are in modern editions of the *Methodist Hymn Book* and also make their appearance in Baptist and Anglican collections (P 34).

Anne Brontë's novels, *Agnes Grey* and *The Tenant of Wildfell Hall*, are better known but have yet to receive the recognition they deserve. They are remarkable both in subject matter and technique. In *Agnes Grey*, Anne developed the governess story in ways which were to influence Charlotte significantly in the writing of both *Jane Eyre* and *Villette*. The younger sister first recognised narrative potential inherent in the story of an intelligent and discriminating, yet obscure, young woman who is placed in a scene of responsibility where she perceives her situation in a substantially different way than others do. *The Tenant of Wildfell Hall* is distinctive in breaking dramatically from this first focus to explore the radical subject of a wealthy wastrel's dissipation and his wife's desperate and disobedient flight into hiding from him.

The technique of both novels is as innovative as the subject matter. In *Agnes Grey*, Anne employed a first-person, female narrator who intimately addresses the 'Reader'. She seems therein to have suggested these new possibilities to Charlotte who, previous to *Jane Eyre*, had never employed a female narrator, even in her juvenilia.[2] In *The Tenant*, Anne uses multiple storytellers and embedded narratives. In this she may have been following Emily's *Wuthering Heights*, but she employs the technique (as we shall see in Chapter 5) to very different ends. In both novels, a privileging of the woman as narrator allows Anne to create a female reality formerly uncharted in novels. Male writers such as Samuel Richardson (*Pamela* and *Clarissa*) and Daniel Defoe (*Moll Flanders* and *Roxana*) had employed female narrators, and women writers like Jane Austen and Fanny Burney had used third-person narrators who took a female point of view, but women writers had not yet claimed for themselves the authority of speaking directly through a woman as narrator. It allowed new freedoms for developing the woman's perspective in the world.

In these achievements, Anne was certainly an innovator. Still, we can trace the influence of earlier writers on her artistic development. We shall first look at Anne

Brontë's literary predecessors, then examine her literary
relationship to Emily and Charlotte, and finally detail her
contributions to the genres of poetry and fiction.

## I

Anne Brontë's literary precursors are significantly different
from those of her sisters. Whereas they were drawn to the
Romantic poets and to writers like Sir Walter Scott, of
whom Charlotte said, 'all novels after his are worthless'
(LL I 122), Anne clearly retained a strong interest in
writers of the eighteenth century: poets, novelists, and
essayists. Her religious preoccupations led her to model
her verse on the poetry and hymns of such writers as
William Cowper, Thomas Moore, and Charles Wesley.
Cowper was an especial favourite, in whose work Brontë
found echoed her own religious preoccupations and questions. Yet in her insistence on universal salvation, Brontë
diverged sharply from Cowper, a strict Calvinist given to
fits of melancholy over his possible damnation.

Brontë may have been attracted to more than Cowper's
religious musings. He wrote thoughtful poems about nature
and everyday life, poems in which emotions often imbue the
description, and so may have provided a model for Brontë's
introspective nature poems in which we also hear echoes of
Thomas Gray, James Thomson, and the Romantic poets.
Poems such as 'The North Wind', 'To a Bluebell', 'Lines
Written at Thorp Green', 'Consolation', 'Home', 'Memory',
'Fluctuations', 'The Arbour', and 'Self-Communion' all use
the natural scene as a starting point for inner reflection.

Anne also had an ear for the music of verse, and would
replicate, perhaps unconsciously, the tone and cadences
of poets like Wordsworth. For example, in her poem
'Dreams', which begins:

While on my lonely couch I lie
I seldom feel myself alone,
For fancy fills my dreaming eye
With scenes and pleasures of its own. (P 113)

We hear Wordsworth's 'Daffodils':

For oft, when on my couch I lie
In vacant or in pensive mood,
They flash upon that inward eye
Which is the bliss of solitude;
And then my heart with pleasure fills,
And dances with the daffodils.

Brontë's subject does not imitate Wordsworth's; her focus
(a young woman's longing for a child) is entirely different,
but his cadences echo in that inward ear.

Although Anne seems to have been less attracted to –
and even critical of – other Romantic poets like Byron
and Shelley (Emily's and Charlotte's favourites), she could
still echo them on occasion. In one poem, distinctive in
its bouyancy, Anne weds the anapaestic tetrameter line
common to Byron with a content reminiscent of Shelley
in 'Ode to the West Wind'. Brontë begins:

My soul is awakened, my spirit is soaring,
And carried aloft on the wings of the breeze;
For, above, and around me, the wild wind is roaring
Arousing to rapture the earth and the seas. (P 88)

The lilting metre captures beautifully the speaker's soaring
spirits which mirror the rapture of the natural scene, as
the wind, arousing the earth and the seas, also arouses
the speaker.

Perhaps the most persistent influence on Anne's work
was the Bible. She knew it thoroughly and drew freely

upon its content and imagery. Given Anne's interest in the Bible as a guide to life, we should not be surprised to find her also drawn to religious stories. John Bunyan's *Pilgrim's Progress* was a favourite of all the Brontës, and we can discern its influence both in Anne's poetic imagery and in the structuring of her novels, particularly *Agnes Grey*. In the poems, Anne Brontë was repeatedly drawn to the final scene from *Pilgrim's Progress* in which Christian, accompanied by Hopeful, must cross the River of Death which divides him from the blessed shore and the gates to the Celestial City. In Anne's poems, the images of the river and shore became potent metaphors, expressing both the difficulty of the challenge and the immensity of the reward. In 'The Three Guides', the speaker argues against the spirit of Earth:

> And pausing by the river's side,
>     Poor reasoner, thou wilt deem,
> By casting pebbles in its tide
>     To cross the swelling stream. (P 146)

Of course, only faith is efficacious in the final challenge for Christian who discovers ground to stand upon when he calls upon Christ.

In 'Self-Communion', the speaker employs the same imagery to describe the bourne she seeks:

> And let me see that sunny shore,
>     However far away!
> However side this rolling sea,
> However wild my passage be. (P 160)

Finally, in 'Views of Life', we find the most developed reference to this scene. The last two stanzas draw persistently on the images from *The Pilgrim's Progress*:

And though that awful river flows
Before us when the journey's past,
Perchance of all the pilgrim's woes
Most dreadful, shrink not – tis the last!

Though icy cold, and dark, and deep;
Beyond it smiles that blessed shore
Where none shall suffer, none shall weep,
And bliss shall reign for evermore. (P 119)

Important as these images are to Anne's poetry, we find
that *Pilgrim's Progress* has a more substantial, although more
subtle influence, on the novels where it shapes the structure
and themes of *Agnes Grey* and *The Tenant of Wildfell Hall*.

That shape is determined not only by Bunyan's story
but also by moral tales like Samuel Johnson's *Rasselas*
and Oliver Goldsmith's *The Vicar of Wakefield*. Although
the 'vanitas' theme is a common one, and Brontë may
have encountered it elsewhere, she seems to have modelled
one of her poems, 'Vanitas Vanitatis', on Johnson's 'The
Vanity of Human Wishes'. *Rasselas*, of course, is Johnson's
prose version of that theme, which both of Brontë's novels
explore. The ideas are summarised in Brontë's poem:

'Tis endless labour everywhere,
Sound cannot satisfy the ear,
Sight cannot fill the craving eye,
Nor riches happiness supply,
Pleasure but doubles future pain;
And joy brings sorrow in her train,
Laughter is mad, and reckless mirth,
What does she in this weary earth? (P 123)

As Agnes Grey goes from her humble home first to the
wealthy Bloomfields' and then to the wealthier Murrays',

and finally witnesses her pupil as the very wealthy but miserable Lady Ashby, she learns the vanity of human wishes. In *The Tenant of Wildfell Hall,* all of Huntingdon's riches cannot satisfy his restlessness and his pleasures seem only to culminate in his damnation. The 'imbecile laughter', described above, sounds throughout the novel (TWH 290).

Anne Brontë shares with Johnson a tendency toward aphoristic statement, which is a product of her moral emphasis. She even fashions some of her sentences with Johnsonian balance. We hear echoes of Rasselas's prose – for example, 'Marriage has many pains, but celibacy has no pleasures'[3] – in Agnes Grey's reflections: 'Though riches had charms, poverty had no terrors for an inexperienced girl like me' (AG 6), or 'To the difficulty of preventing him from doing what he ought not, was added that of forcing him to do what he ought' (AG 22). Brontë's aphorisms differ from Johnson's, however, in their scope. Brontë's apply to a personal situation and are not generalised. And consistent with this difference, Brontë also departs from Johnson, in creating a realistic world with credible, individualised characters. Johnson's *Rasselas* is an apologue designed to point out the impossibility of earthly happiness: its scenes and characters are generalised. Its representation of reality is subordinated to a didactic intent. In contrast, Brontë's themes are subordinated to the reality of presentation. 'Truth' of representation was always Anne's goal, and verisimilitude justified the depiction of sordid individuals and events in *The Tenant*: 'For truth always conveys its own moral to those who are able to receive it' (TWH 29). Brontë argued forcefully in the Preface to *The Tenant of Wildfell Hall* that:

> when we have to do with vice and vicious characters, I maintain it is better to depict them as they really are than as they would wish to appear. To represent a bad thing in its least offensive light is doubtless the most agreeable course for a writer of fiction to pursue; but

is it the most honest, or the safest? . . . Oh, Reader!
if there were less of this delicate concealment of facts,
there would be less of sin and misery to the young of
both sexes, who are left to wring their bitter knowledge
from experience (TWH 30).

Brontë's fiction is distinctive in its yoking of a strong
moral end with an absolute fidelity to representing reality
as she saw it. This moral emphasis, so different from
her sisters', may partially account for her less favourable
reception. And, again, it links her with the eighteenth
century in its insistence that art should both instruct and
entertain, should contain the *dulce* and the *utile*. But if this
moral focus links Brontë with earlier writers, her particular execution of these ends (with the strong insistence on
'less . . . delicate concealment of facts') also sets her apart
from eighteenth-century models like Johnson. In wedding
explicit representation of Huntingdon's debauchery with
moral emphasis, Anne Brontë was charting her own course.

The distinctions between Anne and her better known
sisters continue in the emphasis Anne puts on spiritual
development. The goals of an Anne Brontë protagonist are
to cultivate the spirit and to learn self-command or control
as ways of lessening one's vulnerability to the vicissitudes of
life. Anne may be influenced here by Goldsmith's *The Vicar
of Wakefield*, by other eighteenth-century models, or simply
by the Latin models she studied with Branwell in which
the *vince teipsum* or 'conquer thyself' theme often appears.
Anne's novels inevitably contrast disciplined individuals
with those whose passions are indulged and unregulated.
*Agnes Grey* is a remarkable female protagonist because
the cultivation of the spiritual life leads to self-command
rather than to the self-suppression typical of many other
nineteenth-century female characters like Charlotte's Helen
Burns or George Eliot's Maggie Tulliver. We shall examine
this aspect of Anne's novel more fully in Chapter 4. But

it should be clear at this point that Anne's affinity for eighteenth-century models and themes would cause her work to differ significantly from that of Charlotte and Emily.

Anne Brontë's debt to eighteenth-century models gives her novels an affinity to Jane Austen's although the extent of direct influence is unclear. It seems likely that Anne was simply writing out of the same tradition that shaped Austen and other earlier female authors like Maria Edgeworth and Susan Ferrier. However, we do know that Charlotte read Jane Austen's *Pride and Prejudice* early in 1848, and it seems likely that Anne would have read the novel, too, because all the sisters were together at Haworth. Charlotte's response is recorded in a letter to G. H. Lewes on January 12. It expresses a confirmed dislike which intensified with further acquaintance:

> I had not seen 'Pride and Prejudice' till I read that sentence of yours, and then I got the book. And what did I find? An accurate, daguerreotyped portrait of a commonplace face; a carefully fenced, highly cultivated garden, with neat borders and delicate flowers; but no glance of a bright, vivid physiognomy, no open country, no fresh air, no blue hill, no bonny beck. (LL II 179)

Charlotte's response is unlikely to be Anne's, however, as we find the younger sister echoing Austen in the novel she was currently writing: *The Tenant of Wildfell Hall*. The female protagonist announces: 'my affections not only *ought* to be founded on approbation, but they will and must be so: for without approving I cannot love. It is needless to say I ought to be able to respect and honour the man I marry as *well* as love him, for I cannot love him without' (TWH 150–51). The Austenian balance of reason and passion is endorsed in Anne's novel. Later she counsels a young friend: 'When I tell you not to marry *without* love, I do not advise you to marry for love alone

– there are many, many other things to be considered. Keep both heart and hand in your own possession, till you see good reason to part with them' (TWH 380). As alien as this 'rational' approach to affairs of the heart was to Charlotte, it was just as clearly reasonable, if not always attainable, to Anne. Like Austen, Anne felt that the feelings should not approve a match at which the mind revolted.

Certainly Anne Brontë's emphasis on educating women to develop their capacities for reason proves similar to emphases in earlier women writers and, indeed, links all of these writers with the Enlightenment feminism of the late eighteenth century, which defined Reason as the supreme guide to conduct and argued for the subjection of sexual passion to rational restraint.[4] None of these writers could have hailed Mary Wollstonecraft as a progenitor because of the scandal that erupted upon Godwin's publication of his *Memoirs of the Author of A Vindication of the Rights of Woman* and of Wollstonecraft's letters to Gilbert Imlay. Nonetheless *A Vindication of the Rights of Women* expressed their beliefs succinctly. We shall look in Chapter 5 at the remarkable similarity between Anne Brontë's comments in *The Tenant of Wildfell Hall* and Wollstonecraft's in *A Vindication*. Here we should simply note that Brontë's position on the moral nature and status of women and on female education bears striking similarities to those expressed by Wollstonecraft. At the heart of both writers is the conviction that, if women have immortal souls, then they must be educated in the proper and rational exercise of virtue.

It should be clear that Anne Brontë's religious questionings, her intense religious self-examination, could have produced both the conviction of women's capacity for reason and the ongoing interrogation of the relationship between reason and passion without any direct influences. In her religiosity, Brontë simply returned to the source from which these earlier thinkers had sprung. Yet we do know that in 1843 Anne Brontë purchased Hannah More's *Moral Sketches of Prevailing Opinions and Manners.* More was a contemporary of Wollstonecraft, and, although an arch-conservative, she shared with the more famous feminist 'a strong concern with religion and morals, and a wish to foster moral principles and conduct in female Christians'.[5] Although More dissociated herself from any feminist intention, she seems to have read and been influenced by Wollstonecraft's *Vindication.* More argued for female education on religious grounds and was reluctant to discern any radical political ends in her argument. She, as Anne Brontë would do, grounded her arguments in religion and carefully wedded any intellectual distinction with the religious sensibility. This description that More provides of a particularly eminent woman and her letters might easily be a description of Helen Graham and her diary in *The Tenant of Wildfell Hall:*

> Many specimens of epistolary writing might be produced, which excel these in the graces of composition, but few which surpass them in that strong sense, solid judgment, and those discriminating powers which were the characteristics of her intellectual attainments, as heroic fortitude, Christian humility, unshaken trust in God, and submission to his dispensations, were of her religious character. Such a combination of tenderness the most exquisite, magnanimity the most unaffected, and Christian piety the most practical, have not often met in the same mind.[6]

The yoking of powers of mind with religious fortitude allowed women writers to put forward highly radical arguments in favour of women's equality.

And, of course, once one argues the case for women's education on any grounds, one is already proposing a radical revision of the social code which is built upon the notion of women's inherent inferiority to men in point of intellect and reason. Once the inferiority has been reduced to a mere question of physical strength, the really significant battles have been fought. And these battles were being fought first by Mary Wollstonecraft and later by Anne Brontë, whose representation of domestic abuse in *The Tenant of Wildfell Hall* recalls Wollstonecraft's *Maria*.

## II

Even a cursory glance at the foregoing group of writers who influenced Anne will reveal individuals with whom Charlotte and Emily Brontë would have had little sympathy. It should not surprise us, then, that when the sisters reunited at Haworth in 1845, the former intimacy was not easily resumed. Differences of temperament had been enlarged with the very different experiences each had had during the past several years. While the sisters obviously had an enormous influence on each other, that influence manifests itself as much in difference as in similarity. The stimulation of three highly creative minds was incalculably profitable to each, but it led, in part, to a sharp awareness of how they had diverged philosophically. We shall do most justice to each sister if we acknowledge the differences rather than persist in a romantic myth of oneness. And feminism is best served when we recognise, as we must in the Brontës, that three women could support each other emotionally in all their endeavours despite strong philosophical disagreements about the nature of women and men and about the importance of reason, faith, and passion.

The publication of the poems in 1846 forced the sisters to recognise just how divided they were in purpose and desire. Although Anne apparently tried to heal the breach between Charlotte and Emily, which opened when Charlotte discovered Emily's private poetry and urged publication, nonetheless their divergent perspectives became

increasingly insistent. Indeed, a more realistic picture of
the Brontë sisters at this period paints them as engaged
in forceful dialogues rather than united in a sympathy
that some were better at expressing than others. We shall
spend some time examining the influences among the sisters
because we need to revise the Brontë myth of visionary
Emily, passionate Charlotte, and subdued Anne before we
can truly rehabilitate Anne's reputation.

As she realised the implications of Emily's and Charlotte's
art, Anne seems finally to have wanted to argue against
them. Emily had completed *Wuthering Heights*, Anne *Agnes
Grey*, and Charlotte *The Professor* and most of *Jane Eyre*
when Anne wrote 'The Three Guides', a strong critique
of her sisters' perspectives. Whereas writing for the family
members had been an intimate, private matter, it seems
that Anne suddenly realised that the essence of publication was making public a vision and a truth. She had
been increasingly developing autonomy and individuality
marked by both emotional and aesthetic distance from her
sisters. Their visions of human life must have shocked
Anne, given what we know of her personal religious query
and quest. And, having admitted those criticisms of Charlotte's and Emily's philosophies to herself, her own urge
toward the fullest truth would have made imperative a
responsibility to illuminate the self-indulgent and romantic
bias in her sisters' novels.

'The Three Guides', as I suggested above, is the first
of Anne's works to formalise her critique. In it, a persona considers three spirits – those of Earth, Pride and
Faith – as spiritual guides. She rejects Earth and Pride
and chooses Faith, of 'lowly mien' who represents humble
submission before God and reliance upon divine mercy.
Faith seems to embody Anne's beliefs, expressed elsewhere
in her meditative verse and in her novels. Muriel Spark was
the first to suggest that in the 'Spirit of Pride' Anne was
possibly guying the Byronic arrogance in Emily's Gondal

poems and *Wuthering Heights*, but critics have been unable to account for the 'Spirit of Earth'.

I would like to suggest that the 'Spirit of Earth' provides a profound and subtle echo of Charlotte's St John Rivers from *Jane Eyre*. That Anne was attacking the literary work Charlotte produced and not Charlotte herself does not seem to have occurred to critics although, following Muriel Sparks's lead, they do not hesitate to recognise that the representation of Pride recalls Heathcliff. For example, Edward Chitham notes that, 'In Anne's poem Pride is said to have strong wings and eyes like lightning, just as Heathcliff's are those of a basilisk. The eyes of Pride are "fascinating", but it is a "false destructive blaze"'. And he adds that 'Heathcliff's remark that "the more the worms writhe the more I long to stamp out their entrails" may be echoed in stanza 12 of Anne's poem with its "Cling to the earth, poor grovelling worm!"'[7]

Notably Anne wrote 'The Three Guides' on August 11, 1847, the very month that Charlotte completed *Jane Eyre*. The novel's characters must have been compellingly immediate to Anne. If Emily's Heathcliff was troubling with his arrogance and disdain for a 'coward and fool!' for those of 'timid foot and eye' who cannot 'mount aloft/The steepy mountain-side . . . And gazing from below/[Behold] thy lightning in their eye,/Thy triumph on their brow' (P 146-147), then equally troubling from another perspective must have been Charlotte's St John Rivers, whose cold and steely determination is accompanied by his arrogant conviction of rectitude and infallibility. Humility and human fallibility were the cornerstones of Anne's religious beliefs, and St John's wilful coercion of Jane to his missionary ends must have impressed Anne as dangerous to human happiness and heavenly reward alike. It is true that Jane refuses St John's offer – or rather flees from him to Rochester – but what he represents is endorsed, if not in Jane's fate, then in the resolution of the novel where he, 'the

good and faithful servant', is given the last word: 'His is
the ambition of the high master-spirit, which aims to fill a
place in the first rank of those who are redeemed from the
earth – who stand without fault before the throne of God'.

If we listen, from this perspective, to the opening stanza
of 'The Three Guides', the parallels fairly leap from the
page. Anne Brontë writes:

> Spirit of earth! thy hand is chill.
>> I've felt its icy clasp;
> And shuddering I remember still
>> That stony-hearted grasp
> Thine eye bids love and joy depart,
>> O turn its gaze from me!
> It presses down my sinking heart; –
>> I will not walk with thee!

Charlotte Brontë has described St John as 'hard', 'a cold,
hard man', a 'glacier', 'icy'; he is also stone and metal,
a 'rock firmset in the depths of a restless sea', 'chiselled
marble', 'no longer flesh, but marble', a man dispensing
'marble kisses, or ice kisses', 'inexorable as death'. He asks
that Jane relinquish her will and follow him. He has told her
she is 'formed for labour – not for love' or joy. She believes
the 'insignificant' should 'keep out of his way; lest in his
progress, he should trample them down'.St John represents
a devotion to God that is cheerless, cold, and hard.[8]

In *Jane Eyre*'s final description of St John as a 'master-
spirit . . . redeemed from the earth', Anne has found 'ambition' and the arrogance of purported faultlessness, precisely
the qualities that confine him to the earth – an absolute
reliance on his own judgment, an unquestioning conviction of his rectitude. St John values his understanding;
he asserts, 'Reason, not feeling, is my guide.' And Anne
echoes him in her spirit's assertion that 'Wisdom is mine'
(P 144) and in that spirit's insensitive rationalism. And

her final critique focuses on the inadequacy of his reason
and inexorable will as a guide to salvation:

Striving to make thy way by force,
    Toil-spent and bramble torn,
Thou'lt fell the tree that stops thy course,
    And burst through briar and thorn;
And pausing by the river's side,
    Poor reasoner, thou wilt deem,
By casting pebbles in its tide
    To cross the swelling stream.

Right through the flinty rock thou'lt try
    Thy toilsome way to bore,
Regardless of the pathway nigh
    That would conduct thee o'er.
Not only art thou, then, unkind,
    And freezing cold to me,
But unbelieving, deaf, and blind –
    I will not walk with thee! (P 146)

These stanzas echo the tenor of Jane Eyre's final panegyric
to St John, and, in so doing, mark him as a man motivated
by self-regard, 'unbelieving' in divine mercy. Charlotte
Brontë writes:

A more resolute, indefatigable pioneer never wrought
amidst rocks and dangers. Firm, faithful, and devoted;
full of energy, and zeal, and truth, he labours for his
race: he clears their painful way to improvement: he
hews down like a giant the prejudices of creed and
caste that encumber it. He may be stern; he may be
exacting; he may be ambitious yet; but his is the stern-
ness of the warrior Greatheart . . .[9]

In contrast, Anne presents the spirit of Faith as mild,
loving, and sustaining:

Meek is thine eye and soft thy voice
    But wondrous is thy might
To make the wretched soul rejoice,
    To give the simple light

Even above the tempest's swell,
    I hear thy voice of love,
Of hope and peace I hear them tell,
    And that blest home above.
Through pain and death, I can rejoice,
    If but thy strength be mine.
Earth hath no music like thy voice;
    Life owns no joy like thine! (P 149, 150)

Anne's own sentiments revealed here suggest that she must have been disturbed by a picture of godhead as harsh and exacting as St John's, especially as she was increasingly convinced that salvation was accessible to all, even to apparently abandoned wretches such as Branwell was becoming.

It may be argued that Charlotte Brontë exposes St John and his will-to-power and seemingly discredits him. Yet he remains a potent force in Jane's life and she is ready to 'rush down the torrent of his will into the gulf of his existence, and there lose my own' when she is suddenly 'rescued' by the summoning cry of Rochester.[10] Anne would have censored that masochistic attraction and sought to provide a corrective, alternative model of the religious life.

Anne may have found Charlotte's portrait of Rochester equally dangerous because romantic. Her poem, addressing the question of spiritual guidance, could not touch on Rochester. The novel which she began (probably in January 1848) looks at the secular world. Anne would live only two more years, and her gradual decline must have taught her, in any case, that her time could not be long. She began writing in earnest a second novel, *The Tenant of Wildfell Hall*, a task which she pursued with a zeal that alarmed

Charlotte, who worried about the effect on her health. In letters and in her 'Biographical Notice' to a posthumous reprinting of *Wuthering Heights* and *Agnes Grey*, Charlotte blames *The Tenant of Wildfell Hall* for the rapidity of Anne's decline. She initially notes that its subject was not 'such as the author had pleasure in handling' (LL II 250), and, after Anne's death, she claims categorically that:

> The choice of subject was an entire mistake. Nothing less congruous with the writer's nature could be conceived. The motives which dictated this choice were pure, but, I think, slightly morbid. She had, in the course of her life, been called on to contemplate near at hand, and for a long time, the terrible effects of talents misused and faculties abused; hers was naturally a sensitive, reserved, and dejected nature; what she saw sank very deeply into her mind; it did her harm. She brooded over it till she believed it to be a duty to reproduce every detail (of course with fictitious characters, incidents, and situations) as a warning to others. She hated her work, but would pursue it. When reasoned with on the subject, she regarded such reasonings as a temptation to self-indulgence. She must be honest; she must not varnish, soften, or conceal.[11]

Charlotte's response reveals herself as much as, if not more than, it reveals Anne. Speaking of Anne as morbid, deject-ed, brooding, pursuing work she hated and that did her harm, Charlotte projects onto her sister her own strong distaste for *The Tenant of Wildfell Hall*. Ironically, it was Charlotte who announced, as I noted above, that 'Anne, from her childhood, seemed preparing for an early death' (LL II 338). Thus we may account for the urgency with which Anne wrote as a recognition of the imminence of death, even as she was beginning to emerge as a power-ful writer, someone beginning to discover her purpose on

earth. It is simply impossible to square Charlotte's portrait
of her sister with the persona of the final contemplative
poems or with the implied author of *The Tenant of Wildfell
Hall*. There we find a person of great tenacity, confronting
her destiny, the 'truth', with immense courage.

'Truth' is a constant theme in the writing of both Charlotte and Anne; Emily, in contrast, seems to have felt
no urgency to speak on this subject. The oldest and the
youngest sister, however, were preoccupied by the need
to speak truth. Charlotte announced, 'The Bells are very
sincere in their worship of Truth' (LL II 243). In justifying
her own novels, she argues, 'Unless I can look beyond the
greatest Masters, and study Nature herself, I have no right
to paint. Unless I have the courage to use the language
of Truth in preference to the jargon of Conventionality,
I ought to be silent . . .' (LL II 255). Anne opens *Agnes
Grey* with a similar emphasis, 'All true histories contain
instruction (AG 3)'. In the famous preface to the second
edition of *The Tenant of Wildfell Hall*, she writes:

> My object in writing the following pages was not simply
> to amuse the Reader, neither was it to gratify my own
> taste, nor yet to ingratiate myself with the Press and the
> Public; I wished to tell the truth, for truth always conveys
> its own moral to those who are able to receive it. (TWH 29)

In the light of this equal commitment to truth as a moral
imperative and their different versions of truth, we can
perhaps shed new light on the impulsive rush of Charlotte
and Anne to London to confront Charlotte's publishers
with their separate identities. Anne's publisher, Newby,
in order to boost sales, had been spreading rumours that
*Jane Eyre, Agnes Grey, Wuthering Heights*, and *The Tenant
of Wildfell Hall* were all from the same hand. The insin-
uations impugned Charlotte's integrity because she had
promised her next novel to George Smith. That Charlotte

would feel the matter of some urgency is evident. She wrote to Mary Taylor:

> The upshot of it was that on the very day I received Smith and Elder's letter, Anne and I packed up a small box, sent it to Keighley, set out ourselves after tea, walked through a snowstorm to the station, got to Leeds, and whirled up by the night train to London with the view of proving our separate identity to Smith and Elder, and confronting Newby with his *lie*. (LL II 251)

That Anne would feel an equal urgency that would send the two sisters rushing to London by the next train is less easy to explain. Emily seems to have been indifferent. I would suggest that Anne found personally abhorrent the views expressed in her sisters' novels and distressing their attribution to her. Within days of the visit to London, Anne was writing in her 'Preface' to *Wildfell Hall*: 'One word more, and I have done. Respecting the author's identity, I would have it to be distinctly understood that Acton Bell is neither Currer nor Ellis Bell, and therefore, let not his faults be attributed to them' (TWH 30–31). Or, one might add, let not their faults be attributed to him.

Critics have recently begun to recognise that *Wildfell Hall* is clearly a response to *Wuthering Heights*. The initials of the titular houses – 'W. H.' – are identical. In Emily's novel, we find Heathcliff, Hareton, Hindley; in Anne's Huntingdon, Hattersley, Hargrave, Halford. Both novels used a framed narrative. What kind of response *Wildfell Hall* makes remains in dispute. Jan Gordon argues that 'The publication of *Wuthering Heights* had been a betrayal of the private, albeit communally shared imaginative world of the Brontës. *The Tenant of Wildfell Hall* was a belated attempt to domesticate the damage'.[12] Anne's work is, in this accounting, therefore supplementary to Emily's, a refusal to accept the truths her bolder sister represented. Yet Gordon's reading is once more based on the reliability of Charlotte who states, after her sisters' deaths: 'Anne's character was milder and more subdued . . . She wanted the power, the fire, the originality of her sister, but was well endowed with quiet virtues of her own'.[13]

Edward Chitham provides the most astute analysis of the ways in which Anne is critiquing Emily. He summarises: 'The . . . themes which the novels share include marital unfaithfulness, drunkenness, violence and the question of life after death. On all these topics the sisters occupy very different positions, and it is hard not to see Anne's novel as a corrective to Emily's "soft nonsense"'.[14] Chitham accepts the diverging perspectives between Emily and Anne as a new source of family friction.

Always, critics overlook the inevitable and longstanding friction between Charlotte and Anne, and it can only be because Charlotte had the last word and claimed the upper hand. Charlotte argued that '*Wildfell Hall* it hardly seems to me desirable to preserve' (LL III 156). From Charlotte's perspective, Anne's novel was a 'mistake': 'it was too little consonant with the character, tastes, and ideas of the gentle, retiring, inexperienced writer. She wrote it under a strange, conscientious, half-ascetic notion of accomplishing a painful penance and a severe duty' (LL III 156). When we add to these comments the fact that Charlotte's distaste for *The Tenant of Wildfell Hall* kept it out of print for the duration of Charlotte's life – that is, for ten years after Anne's death – we must conclude that Charlotte could have done little more to destroy her youngest sister's reputation for posterity.

In saying this, I am doing little more than echoing George Moore. But what George Moore did *not* note, and no subsequent critic has remarked, is that Charlotte felt threatened by her sister's novel and its truths. I find it ironic that W. S. Williams, the reader for Charlotte's publishers, was immediately struck by the resemblance between Huntingdon (*The Tenant*'s hero) and Rochester (*Jane Eyre*'s hero) and wrote to Charlotte to that effect. She responded emphatically:

You say Mr. Huntingdon reminds you of Mr. Rochester. Does he? Yet there is no likeness between the
two: the foundation of each character is entirely different. Huntingdon is a specimen of the naturally selfish,
sensual, superficial man, whose one merit of a joyous
temperament only avails him while he is young and
healthy, whose best days are his earliest, who never
profits by experience, who is sure to grow worse the
older he grows. Mr. Rochester has a thoughtful nature
and a very feeling heart; he is neither selfish nor self-
indulgent; he is ill-educated, misguided; errs, when he
does err, through rashness and inexperience: he lives for
a time as too many other men live, but being radically
better than most men, he does not like that degraded
life, and is never happy in it. He is taught the severe
lessons of experience and has sense to learn wisdom
from them. Years improve him; the effervescence of
youth foamed away, what is really good in him still
remains. His nature is like wine of a good vintage, time
cannot sour, but only mellows him. (LL II 244–45)

Charlotte's self-assessment – so favourable to *her* creation –
has been allowed to stand, and Williams' early recognition
of consanguinity between Rochester and Huntingdon has
not been repeated. But because Huntingdon *followed* Rochester, Williams would have been more justified in asking
Anne about the intertextual resemblances. And we may
discover evidence that Charlotte implicitly recognised the
relationship of Huntingdon to Rochester in that she denies
her later heroes the massive sensual appeal of a Rochester
and, in painting Robert Moore and M. Paul, returns to
the autocratic probity of her professor, Crimsworth.

Let me summarise briefly pertinent aspects of the plots
of *Jane Eyre* and *The Tenant of Wildfell Hall*. At the core
of both stories is the romance between a naive and innocent
young woman, Jane and Helen respectively, and an older

man, Rochester and Huntingdon, experienced in the world
and partly corrupted by it. Both women are seen and see
themselves as capable of redeeming the barrenness and
waste of the man's earlier life, a life in which inadequate
education has left him prey to certain vices and vicious
tendencies. But, while Jane Eyre is poor, obscure, and
plain, Helen Graham is rich, prominent, and beautiful. The
contrast suggests that Anne Brontë wanted to make explicit
that, with all the advantages in the world, no woman can
easily reform a man whose habits are already established; far
less can she undertake that task if she has the disadvantage
of social inferiority. Helen marries her Huntingdon at the
commencement of her story and is brought to a painful
realisation of her foolish idealism. For Helen, marriage
is the beginning of growth; for Jane it marks the end.
Jane Eyre's marriage to Rochester culminates her fairy tale
romance, as Charlotte's book must have seemed to Anne,
a story wildly at odds with Anne's extensive and intimate
experience at Thorp Green with the gentlemanly class.

Both Rochester and Huntingdon are sexually incontinent.
Rochester's name recalls the dissolute John Wilmot, Earl
of Rochester. Perhaps in parody, Anne creates a minor
character named Wilmot, 'a worthless old reprobate' (TWH
154). More pertinent, the woman with whom Huntingdon
commits adultery is Annabella Wilmot, this man's niece.
Annabella Wilmot also echoes the name of a character
in The Vicar of Wakefield, a pure and loyal woman who
provides a contrast to Anne Brontë's corrupt character.
Charlotte's Rochester has 'tried dissipation' as a means of
forgetting he is wedded to a madwoman.[15] Jane arrives at
Thornfield as his redemptive angel. Rochester describes
Jane in the exact terms that Helen Graham conceives her
role with Huntingdon: 'You are my sympathy – my better self – my good angel – I am bound to you with a
strong attachment'.[16] Huntingdon, too, speaks of Helen
as his 'angel' (TWH 163, 185). Rochester says of Jane:

After a youth and manhood passed half in unutterable misery and half in dreary solitude, I have for the first time found what I truly love – I have found *you* . . . I am bound to you with a strong attachment. I think you good, gifted, lovely: a fervent, a solemn passion is conceived in my heart; it leans to you, draws you to my centre and spring of life, wraps my existence about you.[17]

As if in echo, Huntingdon claims:

My father, you know, was something of a miser, and in his later days especially, saw no pleasure in life but to amass riches; and so it is no wonder that his son should make it his chief delight to spend them, which was accordingly the case, until my acquaintance with you, dear Helen, taught me other views and nobler aims. And the very idea of having you to care for under my roof would force me to moderate my expenses and live like a Christian – not to speak of all the prudence and virtue you would instil in my mind by your wise counsels and sweet, attractive goodness. (TWH 188)

These passages, so similar in idea yet so different in style and tone, point to the contrasting intentions of their authors. Anne Brontë's Helen attempts to fulfill the role of redemptive angel and fails miserably because her author refuses the consolatory notion that rooted, evil tendencies can be eradicated by the influence of an angelic young lady.

Both novels' protagonists, Jane and Helen, are forced to flee the immorality in which they find themselves almost enmeshed. Both women thrive by the fruits of their own labour, and both ultimately return to the estates they have fled, Thorn-field and its echo, with a difference, Grassdale. For Anne, redemption is possible only in heaven; Huntingdon is dying. Any reformation on earth would

seem to be a foolish girl's foolish dream. In *Jane Eyre*,
of course, the romance of earthly redemption is enacted
in Jane's marriage to Rochester.

This summary, brief as it is, reveals the critique of
Charlotte's novel inherent in Anne's. But *The Tenant of
Wildfell Hall* would not be so good a novel as it is if it
were content to stay at this level. As in other great novels
where one writer sets out to correct another – Fielding's
*Joseph Andrews* as revision of Richardson's *Pamela* is only
the most famous example – the initial impulse gives way
to a larger, more comprehensive vision. So Anne's novel
establishes its own reality and psychological complexity. In
Chapter 5 I shall present those grounds on which we may
claim independent excellence for *The Tenant of Wildfell
Hall*. In its combination of unblinking social realism with
intense religious questioning, it produces a brilliant synthesis in vision, one imbued with a profound sense of
the ongoing dialectic between the fleshly and spiritual,
between the quotidian and transcendent.

## III

We have considered at length the intertextual relationships
among the Brontë novels because that intertextuality is highly illuminating, allowing us new insights into Anne's work
and making evident her influence on Charlotte. The vexed
relationship between *Wildfell Hall* and *Jane Eyre* also helps
explain the disappearance of *Wildfell Hall* from print for ten
years and its absence as literary influence in the later decades
of the nineteenth century. Had the novel been more widely
available, it might have helped generate representations of
a new kind of heroine, more spirited and independent.

The autonomy of Anne Brontë's heroines is truly compelling. She gives us protraits of women prepared to support
themselves in the world, women who are independent of

male approval and who are content without male attention. Portrait after portrait by women novelists of the Victorian period gives us the opposite: women characters emotionally dependent on male approval and attention. Although those same women novelists present the powerful truth that women have dual, and seemingly incompatible, needs for both relationship with a man and independence from patriarchal restrictions (which may be embodied in that man), Anne Brontë, with another focus, gives us equally powerful and affirming portraits of women who have sufficient self-confidence and autonomy (financial and emotional) that they can ultimately command the terms of relationship. And if the man fails to meet those terms, they will simply walk away. Their need for self-respect and autonomy wins out over their need for relationship and so reverses the usual hierarchy for women where the relationship supersedes independence. It seems likely, therefore, that the evolution of Charlotte's heroines – from the extremely pliant Frances of *The Professor,* through rebellious Jane, bold Shirley Keeldar, and independent Lucy Snowe – registered in some degree the impact of Anne's Agnes Grey and Helen Graham.

If Charlotte Brontë was radical in claiming a sexual identity for women,[18] then Anne Brontë was radical in claiming a professional identity for women. Agnes Grey and her mother succeed at opening a school, perhaps providing a model for Charlotte's Lucy Snowe in *Villette.* Helen Graham Huntingdon supports herself with her painting. She confounds community expectation on several levels.[19] First, she openly invites unexpected visitors into her studio. They confess their amazement:

> To our surprise, we were ushered into a room where the first object that met the eye was a painter's easel, with a table beside it covered with rolls of canvas, bottles of oil and varnish, palette, brushes, paints, etc. Leaning

against the wall were several sketches in various stages of progression, and a few finished paintings – mostly of landscapes and figures. (TWH 68)

Far from wishing to conceal her occupation, Helen behaves as a man would in comparable circumstances. She tacitly displays her sense of interruption by continuing to paint:

> And disengaging a couple of chairs from the artistical lumber that usurped them, she bid us be seated, and resumed her place beside the easel – not facing it exactly, but now and then glancing at the picture upon it while she conversed, and giving it an occasional touch with her brush, as if she found it impossible to wean her attention entirely from her occupation to fix it upon her guests. (TWH 68)

Gilbert Markham, one of the visitors, is compelled to admit that the picture is 'very elegantly and artistically handled', and he betrays his masculine sensitivity toward feminine accomplishment in the admission that he surveyed the painting 'with a greater degree of admiration and delight than I cared to express'. (TWH 68) Of course, Markham is being called upon to revise several conventional notions of the woman painter: first, that she paints from a finishing school pattern and second, that she paints as a social adornment not as economic necessity. When Markham asks, 'Then you don't intend to keep the picture?', Helen responds, 'No; I cannot afford to paint for my own amusement.' Helen's son reveals that she supports them with her art. (TWH 69) Throughout the novel, Helen is practical and professional in her painting, even offending Gilbert Markham by her 'evident desire to be rid of [him]' while she is sketching. (TWH 89)

Anne Brontë is also an innovator in her depiction of masculine weakness, just evident in the self-satisfied irritation of Gilbert Markham. Women's literature of the nineteenth century has provided numerous models of male tyranny and vanity – portraits that stem from male abuse of patriarchal power. But Anne Brontë's portraits differ; they stress moral debility and irrationality. Her male characters are not capable of tyranny. Huntingdon is finally a whining, whimpering, frightened wretch; Gilbert Markham is given to bouts of violence that are revealed to be as irrational as they are dangerous. Women writers do not often depict physical violence in men but, when they do, the power revealed commands respect. Emily Brontë's Heathcliff is feared for his physical abuses; Charlotte Brontë's Robert Moore from *Shirley* elicits awe from the women when he 'speaks' through guns in quelling the Luddite rioters. In contrast, when Gilbert Markham assaults the innocent Frederick Lawrence, who tries to turn away his wrath with mildness and reason, he is made to appear a madman. He briefly worries – 'Had I killed him?' – and then rationalises his action absurdly: 'it would teach him better manners in future' (TWH 134). Similarly, the domestic violence in Helen's life with Huntingdon inspires only contempt not fear. When one man coerces his wife by 'remorsely crushing her slight arms in the grip of his powerful fingers', Helen fearlessly calls upon the woman's brother to intercede on her behalf and, when he doesn't, she confronts the brutal man. She is revolted by her own husband's degradation and sees him as 'sick and stupid' (TWH 291).

Not only does Anne Brontë thus revise our awe at male physical strength, she exhibits in her heroines no symptoms of attraction to that violence.[20] Whereas a Charlotte Brontë heroine will 'often respond in a disturbingly masochistic way to masculine aggression',[21] an Anne Brontë heroine is revolted by the abuse of strength. She does not seek a master; she seeks a partner. Agnes initially describes her sister's husband to her pampered charges as a 'middling' sort of man, and they expostulate, like true romantic heroines, 'O stop! – you'll make me sick. How *can* she bear it?' (AG 60). Agnes replies, 'I expect she'll not only be able to bear it, but to be very happy. You did not ask me if Mr Richardson were a good, wise, or amiable man' (AG 60). Agnes describes her own suitor, Edward Weston, as 'a very *respectable* man', 'a very sensible man', a very unromantic man (AG 155) who does not indulge himself in the 'honied phrases and fervent protestations of most other men' and who refuses to 'talk soft nonsense' and so insult Agnes's intelligence (AG 157). *The Tenant of Wildfeld Hall* becomes a cautionary tale that exposes the foolish romance in the attraction of a Byronic hero like Huntingdon and finally rewards the heroine with a very ordinary gentleman farmer who has had the grace to learn humility.

Anne Brontë also innovates in her choice of heroines both in *Agnes Grey* and in *The Tenant of Wildfell Hall*. Agnes Grey is an ordinary, practical, and undistinguished woman. She possesses neither fortune nor beauty. In short, she has nothing to recommend her to a reader's, or a man's, attention. Yet, by making Agnes narrator of her story, Brontë makes her both attractive and compelling. Anne no doubt pointed the way for Charlotte's Jane Eyre, both in her female narrator and in her poor, plain, and obscure heroine who is capable of rebelling at the humiliations of her situation.

The power of that female narrator is potentially immense, as Anne Brontë seemed to recognise. She organises the narrative and the vision of human reality it presents. She has the power to shape and to revise a reader's expectations and values by explicit appeals to his or her sensibility and intelligence. In short, she is capable of creating, through the medium of fiction, a reader fit to read her story. Brontë began to explore this potential in *Agnes Grey*. Of course, from the beginning the narrator is implicitly begging our indulgence in her tale, but toward the end of the novel, Anne Brontë seemed to realise that she could make those appeals both more direct and more affective by addressing the reader explicitly. So Agnes adopts a personal relationship with her reader:

> I fear, by this time, the reader is well-nigh disgusted with the folly and weakness I have so freely laid before him. I never disclosed it then, and would not have done so had my own sister or my mother been with me in the house. I was a close and resolute dissembler – in this one case at least. My prayers, my tears, my wishes, fears, and lamentations, were witnessed by myself and Heaven alone. (AG 117)

Later, too, when Brontë is revising significantly our notions of what constitutes narrative interest, she lets Agnes address the reader again:

> Well! what is there remarkable in all this? Why have I recorded it! Because, reader, it was important enough to give me a cheerful evening, a night of pleasing dreams, and a morning of felicitous hopes. Shallow-brained cheerfulness, foolish dreams, unfounded hopes, you will say; and I will not venture to deny it: suspicions to that effect arose too frequently in my own mind. But our wishes are like tinder: the flint and steel of circumstances are continually striking out sparks, which vanish immediately, unless they chance to fall upon the tinder of our wishes; then they instantly ignite, and the flame of hope is kindled in a moment. (AG 125)

Women writers often lacked the courage to tell their own stories because they seemed too humble, too domestic, too uninteresting. Anne Brontë's Agnes Grey may have been the first to tell that story and to discover the techniques by which it could win its audience. The gain to Charlotte, the distance between The Professor and Jane Eyre, was immense.

Anne Brontë discovered through *Agnes Grey* the power inherent in allowing a woman to tell her own story and incorporated a woman's story, told in her own words, into *The Tenant of Wildfell Hall*. Through this technique, she accomplished the unprecedented end of transforming the story of a runaway wife and fallen woman into that of exemplary womanhood, an achievement we shall evaluate more fully in Chapter 5.

Finally, it is worth pointing to the psychological sophistication in Anne Brontë's novels. They offer convincing portraits of the mind under duress and subtle analyses of the dynamics of human relationships. Brontë may have been the first to paint a portrait of the father's intense jealousy of his usurping son, and critics have credited Anne with creating in Rosalie Murray (from *Agnes Grey*) the prototype of the indulged, unreasonable, and wealthy flirt that Charlotte picked up in *Villette*'s Ginevra Fanshawe.[22]

Anne Brontë is surely an author worthy of interest in her own right. Her thematic innovations place her in the forefront of feminist thought in the nineteenth century even as her formal and technical innovations demand that we look again at her contributions to the English novel. Both thematic and technical innovations were assimilated into Charlotte's novels and passed on to generations of writers. Perhaps George Moore was right when he claimed that Anne was the sacrifice to make credible the genius of Emily and Charlotte: 'Three phthisis-stricken sisters living on a Yorkshire moor, and all three writing novels, were first-rate copy, and Charlotte's little depreciations of the dead were a great help, for three sisters of equal genius might strain the credulity of the readers of the evening newspapers'.[23] But we must not be bound by the conventional wisdom that reached that conclusion. If there are three geniuses, then we must count them three.

# 3 The Poems: 'pillars of witness'

It may seem that close attention to Anne Brontë's poetic corpus is unwarranted in the light of her status as a very minor poet. Yet because the body of work constitutes the spiritual autobiography of a person for whom we have little other such evidence (as in letters and diaries) and because the lyrics have their own quiet merit, we would distort our understanding of Anne Brontë and continue certain long-standing prejudices against her by failing to give the poems detailed consideration. In addition, in producing a body of verse that continues to find readers, Anne Brontë has placed herself among a very small minority of women poets in the nineteenth century.

It has been common for critics to divide Anne Brontë's poetic output (a total of fifty-nine poems) into two groups: Gondal and non-Gondal. The former, a group of twenty-three poems, was produced almost entirely during periods of close intimacy with Emily. The latter, a group of over thirty poems, represents a spiritual and emotional autobiography that includes love poems, religious and didactic poems, hymns, and introspective and dialogue poems.

In a few poems, the Gondal and non-Gondal merge in content and tone. That such mergings exist should not surprise us. I would like to argue here that even the strictly Gondal poems in Anne's poetic canon – poems signed by Gondal characters – introduce or develop themes that will colour her 'autobiographical' poems. It seems

61

that, inevitably, a poet must impress her personality and preoccupations upon the work she creates, even if she is adopting explicit personas. We may note that dramatic monologues allow a poet to 'tell my state as though 'twere none of mine'.[1] Likewise, we must expect that Anne's Gondal characters took their distinctive colouring from her imagination and gradually revealed to her the resources of poetry for spiritual and emotional self-expression.

As evidence for this conclusion, we may begin with the observation that, between December 1836 and August 1838, Anne wrote eight Gondal poems. Then, on January 1, 1840, she produced one of the hybrid poems with a Gondal signature but with a very Haworthian context. The poem, entitled 'A Fragment', is in the form of a dialogue, a technique Anne was to develop with great sophistication in her later works. A maiden is queried by a companion over her change in appearance. The poem begins, 'Maiden, thou wert thoughtless once/Of beauty or of grace' and then the questionner remarks, 'Then whence this change, and why so oft/Dost smooth thy hazel hair?' To deflect further questions, the maiden replies:

Nay, gentle friends, I can but say
    That childhood's thoughts are gone
Each year its own new feelings brings
    And years move swiftly on,

She is relieved that 'They could not read my secret thoughts/ Nor see my throbbing heart', especially since she has known many who lack her skill at concealment. Her triumph lies in the fact that her emotion at the approach of some unnamed man – biographers have suggested that William Weightman is that man – goes undetected:

And yet my comrades marked it not,
    My voice was still the same;

They saw me smile, and o'er my face –
   No signs of sadness came;
They little knew my hidden thoughts
   And they will never know
The anguish of my drooping heart,
   The bitter aching woe! (P 71–72)

This remarkable capacity for emotional concealment seems to have been Anne's as well as the speaker's of this poem. In her long, autobiographical poem, 'Self-Communion', the poet notes that, 'That inner life of strife and tears,/Of kindling hopes and lowering fears,/To none but God is known' (P 154). And may it not have been because Anne was so successful at concealing deep emotion beneath a placid exterior, that Charlotte, who was Anne's first critic, was so inept a reader of her sister's work.

  In this poem Anne reveals not only her capacity for concealment, but also her recognition of the swift passage of time and the changes wrought by time. An idea here presented to deflect further curiosity ironically becomes a poignant theme in the two novels where we shall examine its development in later chapters.

  The point I want to emphasise now is that the Gondal and non-Gondal poems are not thematically divided; they are intimately intertwined as our examination of 'A Fragment' reveals. Nor surprisingly, following this poem Anne went on to write lyrics, without Gondal signature, that reflect her own experience directly. That poetry should serve as such an avenue for self-expression is an idea Anne Brontë develops in *Agnes Grey*. Although we should not make the mistake of conflating Anne with the protagonist of her first novel, it seems reasonable to suggest that Anne reflects her own motives for writing poetry in the thoughts of her character. Agnes Grey writes:

When we are harassed by sorrows or anxieties, or long oppressed by any powerful feelings which we must

keep to ourselves, for which we can obtain and seek no
sympathy from any living creature, and which yet we
cannot or will not wholly crush, we often naturally seek
relief in poetry – and often find it, too – whether in the
effusions of others, which seem to harmonise with our
existing case, or in our own attempts to give utterance
to those thoughts and feelings in strains less musical,
perchance, but more appropriate, and therefore more
penetrating and sympathetic, and, for the time, more
soothing, or more powerful to rouse and to unburden
the oppressed and swollen heart . . . I still preserve
those relics of past sufferings and experience, like
pillars of witness set up in travelling through the
vale of life, to mark particular occurrences. (AG 117)

Anne's poems, like Agnes's are 'pillars of witness' to
her own emotional odyssey, and it is striking, too, that
Agnes articulates the resources of poetry in a context
very similar to the one in which Anne Brontë made
her comparable discovery. Agnes, like the speaker of 'A
Fragment', is practising both the more careful grooming of
her person and the concealment of her emotion described
in Anne's poem 'A Fragment'. Agnes tells us that, 'I may
as well acknowledge that, about this time, I paid more
attention to dress than ever I had done before' (AG
110) and that 'I was used to wearing a placid smiling
countenance when my heart was bitter within me' (AG 116).
Anne Brontë suggests, then, that her protagonist, Agnes
Grey, discovers poetry as a resource for self-expression
much as she herself seems to have recognised its potential.

# I

Yet, the early, 'purely' Gondal poems were the seed
bed for this discovery that poems could be 'pillars of

witness', as Brontë was already planting her particular concerns within the Gondal characters. We shall trace the themes of physical and emotional captivity, of the relations between feeling and perception, of the tensions between hope and experience, of recollection as a way to transcend vicissitudes of time, of the emphemerality of hope imaged in dreams, and of the nature of home and the outlaw.

One prominent interest, carried throughout the poetic career, lay in the idea of captivity. Naturally, the Gondal sagas were full of stories of betrayal and revenge with the attendant dungeon imprisonments. But Anne became fascinated by the possible meanings of such captivity. It may be that Byron's treatment of the theme in the 'Prisoner of Chillon' was colouring her own representations to some extent. Whether she had his poem in mind or not, she clearly grasped two points that are also present in Byron's narrative: first, that captives may suffer more for others than for themselves; and second, that long captivity inures one to one's state and, in the absence of friends to whom one can return upon release, ultimately renders the world a mighty prison. In 'A Voice from the Dungeon', the character dreams of liberty but also of 'tortured friends and happy foes'. Anne's next poem, 'The Captive's Dream', expresses more anguish for the suffering loved ones than for the captive herself: 'O heaven I could bear/My deadly fate with calmness if there were/No kindred hearts to bleed and break for me!' (P 62).

In these Gondal poems, Anne Brontë details a physical restraint that keeps suffering loved ones apart and that threatens to make the world a cold and loveless place. In a later, non-Gondal poem, 'The Captive Dove', Brontë imagines herself as a bird in captivity. The physical restraints on the dove – the 'prison roof' and 'slender wires' – become metaphors for the emotional restraints the persona is forced to practise. The speaker argues that:

Yet hadst thou but one gentle mate
The little drooping heart to cheer
And share with thee thy captive state,
Thou couldst be happy even there. (P 93)

In short, what is truly debilitating about captivity is
that it severs one from the solace of love. There is less
emphasis on the abstract value of liberty than on the
need for loving and nurturing relationships, an emphasis
that contemporary psychoanlytic critics see as distinctively
feminine.[3] Concluding, the speaker laments:

But thou, poor solitary dove,
Must make unheard thy joyless moan;
The heart that nature formed to love
Must pine neglected and alone. (P 93)

Anne Brontë identifies captivity now as a self-enforced
restraint when love cannot be expressed. This context
allows us to see that such restraint is echoed in the
self-concealment of the persona in 'A Fragment'.

These chains of captivity are also images for the self-con-
trol the speaker must continually practise. In 'The Arbour',
the person begins in an optimistic mood anticipating that,
as she listens to the rustle of boughs, 'My winged soul
shall fly away;/Reviewing long departed years/As one mild,
beaming, autumn day'. But she is thwarted as she recognises that the frost in the air is also present in her heart:

And winter's chill is on my heart –
How can I dream of future bliss?
How can my spirit soar away,
Confined by such a chain as this? (P 110–111)

The chain is forged both by long-standing self-restraint
and a growing disillusionment and bitterness with human

affairs. It was shortly after writing this poem that Anne noted in her prayer book: 'Disgusted with mankind and all its ways'.

Because Anne has come to see her own condition as a kind of imprisonment – as inability to escape what she would not see and a failure to express what she needs must feel – it is not surprising that when she returned to Haworth in the summer of 1845 and resumed writing Gondal poetry with Emily, she repeatedly returns to the captive motif. In Anne's poem #48, 'A prisoner in a dungeon deep', we find the poignant acceptance of the permanence of captivity:

No, he has lived so long enthralled
Alone in dungeon gloom
That he has lost regret and hope,
Has ceased to mourn his doom.

He pines not for the light of day
Nor sighs for freedom now;
Such weary thoughts have ceased at length
To rack his burning brow. (P 126)

The captive has ceased to long for freedom because it has become unattainable even were his physical restraints released. When he is suddenly informed that his foes are dead and he is free, he experiences no ecstasy:

My foes are dead! It must be then
That all mankind are gone.
For they were all my deadly foes
And friends I had not one. (P 128)

This is a bitter conclusion that finds the world a prison.

Approximately a year later, Anne could write with greater equanimity, and the Gondal character of #51, 'Weep not too much, my darling', urges her distant love, unconfined by chains, to 'Say that the charms of Nature/Are lovely still to thee' even though the bars of captivity efface the speaker's own view of nature. In a beautiful image, Brontë presents the way in which imprisonment shapes perception:

When through the prison grating
The holy moonbeams shine,
And I am wildly longing
To see the orb divine
Not crossed, deformed, and sullied
By those relentless bars
That will not show the crescent moon,
And scarce the twinkling stars. (P 132)

In 'Self-Communion', completed in April of 1848, Anne sounds a new and positive note: a resolution to break the chains that confine.

Earth hath too much of sin and pain:
The bitter cup – the binding chain
Dost thou indeed lament?
Let not thy weary spirit sink;
But strive – not by one drop or link
The evil to augment.
Strive rather thou, by peace and joy,
The bitter poison to destroy,
The cruel chain to break. (P 159)

It is a fitting conclusion, one that first recognises the extent to which we participate in our captivity by augmenting the links and that subsequently resolves to break the crippling bonds.

As we examined the theme of the captive, we also heard the note of a corollary theme being introduced: the recognition that one's physical and emotional condition colours her perception of the universe. Although this theme never has the epistemological emphasis it receives in Wordsworth and Coleridge – where Anne may have found it in 'Tintern Abbey' ('Both what they [eye and ear] half create,/And what perceive') and in 'Dejection: An Ode' ('O Lady! we receive but what we give,/And in our life alone does Nature live:/Ours is her wedding garment, ours her shroud!') – nonetheless Anne echoes it often enough to suggest that these Romantic ideas resonated in her own sensibility. Again, this theme has its roots in her earliest Gondal poems.

> O why are things so changed to me?
> > What gave me joy before
> Now fills my heart with misery,
> > And nature smiles no more
>
> And why are all the beauties gone
> > From this my native hill?
> Alas! my heart is changed alone:
> > Nature is constant still. (P 50)

The idea that changes occur in the perceiver, not in nature, appears again in #5 'The North Wind': 'The sweet world is not changed, but thou/Art pining in a dungeon now' (P 63).

Brontë's first major dialogue poem, #42, 'Views of Life', begins with this same contrast between the perceiving eye and the outward scene and now her grasp is more secure, her development more sophisticated as she details the conflict between hopeful youth and the experienced adult:

> When sinks my heart in hopeless gloom,
> When life can show no joy for me,
> And I behold a yawning tomb
> Where bowers and palaces should be,
>
> In vain, you talk of morbid dreams,

In vain, you gaily smiling say
That what to me so dreary seems
The healthy mind deems bright and gay. (P 115)

But the view here represented in the last two lines –
that the perceiving eye alters all – belongs to an inexperienced youth. Brontë takes a direction very different from
Wordsworth's and Coleridge's when another, experienced
voice in the poem argues for an objective truth:

So gilded by the glow of youth
Our varied life looks fair and gay,
And so remains the naked truth
When that false light is past away. (P 115)

Now the perceptions of youth are deemed 'false' as the
speaker pursues the idea of a 'naked truth', a conception
no doubt produced by Anne's own religious quests. In
stanzas reminiscent of one of Keats's in 'Ode on a Grecian
Urn', ('All breathing human passion far above,/That leaves
a heart high-sorrowful and cloy'd./A burning forehead,
and a parching tongue'), the mature speaker argues the
transitoriness of human joy:

Fond dreamer! little does she know
The anxious toil, the suffering,
The blasted hopes, the burning woe,
The object of her joy will bring.

As little know the youthful pair
In mutual love supremely blest
What weariness and cold despair
Ere long will seize the aching breast. (P 116)

The sole release from the coils of temporality, for Brontë's
speaker, lies in hope and memory: hope for what may yet
be, memory of what beauty there has been:

No! while we journey on our way,
We'll notice every lovely thing,
And ever as they pass away,
To memory and hope we'll cling. (P 119)

Hope and memory enable us to endure our mortal journey,
the bourne of which is 'that blessed shore/Where none shall
suffer, none shall weep,/And bliss shall reign for evermore'
(P 119). In positing an eternal resting place, Brontë has obviously diverged significantly from Wordsworth, Coleridge,
and Keats. Yet the poem retains a moving power because
she finally refuses, as they do, a simple, temporal 'truth'.
Where the mature speaker initially insists on a 'naked truth',
the dialogue with youth has forced the recognition that
hope, although it may be disappointed, is to be cherished:

Because the road is rough and long,
Shall we despise the skylark's song,
That cheers the wanderer's way?
Or trample down, with reckless feet
The smiling flowerets bright and sweet
Because they soon decay? (P 119)

The mere fact of temporality does not invalidate our
experience, and truth on earth is tied to evanescence.
   The importance of hope and memory to Anne Brontë
emerges early in her poetry and, again, recalls Wordsworth.
But where Wordsworth finds a resource in memory, reflection, and thought when contemplating nature because they
more fully tie him to humanity, because they more fully
acquaint him with the connections among all things ('To
me the meanest flower that grows can give/Thoughts that
do often lie too deep for tears' – 'Intimations Ode'), Anne
Brontë diverges in asserting that we are moved not simply
by memory's power in contemplating nature but by God's

greatness imaged in the universe. In poem #18, 'In Memory of a Happy Day in February', the speaker experiences joy and seeks its source. She dismisses the elements ('Neither sun nor wind/Could raise my spirit so' [P 82]), a common source of motive power for the Romantics (for example, Wordsworth, 'Resolution and Independence', Colderidge, 'Dejection: An Ode', and Shelley, 'Ode to the West Wind'), and identifies 'a glimpse of truths divine/Unto my spirit given'. Finally, the speaker asserts:

But most throughout the moral world
    I saw his glory shine;
I saw his wisdom infinite,
        His mercy all divine. (P 82)

For Brontë, it is God's glory that illuminates the world with moral significance.

Brontë's later poem 'Memory' (#32) returns to this issue in a more complex way. She argues with Wordsworth over the 'divinity' of childhood and the subsequent divine power of memory:

Is childhood then so all divine?
Or, memory, is the glory thine
That haloes thus the past?
Not all divine; its pangs of grief
Although perchance their stay is brief,
Are bitter while they last. (P 102)

Anne's refusal to idealise childhood stems from a very concrete knowledge of children (we may compare *Agnes Grey*), and a keen memory of her own childhood. And her consequent refusal to use memory's power to refashion the past leads Brontë to posit a 'holy light' as a source of the glory.

Nor is the glory all thine own,
For on our earliest joys alone
That holy light is cast.

With such a ray no spell of thine
Can make our later pleasures shine,
Though long ago they passed. (P 102)

In short, memory simply lacks the power to irradiate our
later pleasures even after they have past into the haze of
imperfect recollection. Ironically, although a religious idealist, Brontë is a realist about human affairs and experience,
and in her revisions of Wordsworth makes him appear very
much an idealist in human matters. Perhaps her realistic
disposition helps explain Brontë's power as a novelist.

Yet another theme having its roots in the Gondal poetry
weds memory with fidelity to define recollection of love as
a way to transcend the vicissitudes of time and experience.
It asserts the tenacity, even the permanence of love, even in
the face of acknowledged transience. In Anne Brontë's first
poem, two Gondal characters pledge to meet again, though
severed now, and one exclaims: 'And if you do not meet
me – know/I am not false but dead' (P 55). Alexandrina
Zenobia, another Gondal character, asserts that 'Nothing
short of death could keep/So true a heart from thee' (P
68). And Alexandrina Zenobia claims in a subsequent
poem that, 'This lingering love will not depart/I cannot
banish from my heart/The friend of childish years' (P
70). Or in 'An Orphan's Lament', a Gondal character
identified as A. H. insists:

And parted friends how dear soe'er
Will soon forgotten be;
It may be so with other hearts,
It is not thus with me. (P 78)

We may remark that this emphasis belongs to the stock
and trade of romantic love, but Brontë translates it into a
moving expression of the power of love over circumstances,
time, and death.

Brontë's non-Gondal love poems – those that critics
have associated with her attraction to William Weightman
– assert this same tenacity of feeling that the external world
and time cannot corrupt. In poem #12, the speaker laments:

Oh, they have robbed me of the hope
    My spirit held so dear;
They will not let me hear that voice
    My soul delights to hear. (P 75)

Nonetheless the speaker defeats that world in some measure
through the force of feeling:

Well, let them seize on all they can; –
    One treasure still is mine, –
A heart that loves to think on thee,
    And feels the worth of thine. (P 76)

This same insistence on the ability of fond feelings to
transcend external conditions begins Brontë's next poem:

Farewell to thee! but not farewell
    To all my fondest thoughts of thee:
Within my heart they still shall dwell;
    And they shall cheer and comfort me. (P 76)

The most intense expression of this idea – the permanence
of love in the face of transience – occurs in a relatively late
poem, 55, dated April 1847. We also note the advance in
subtlety and sophistication:

Thou breathest in my bosom yet,
And dwellest in my beating heart;

And, while I cannot quite forget,
Thou, darling, canst not quite depart. (P 143)

The lyric then develops a new dimension of this thesis:
that the presence of this undying love ever after colours
the speaker's perception:

Life seems more sweet that thou didst live,
And men more true that thou wert one:
Nothing is lost that thou didst give,
Nothing destroyed that thou hast done. (P 143)

Finally, in a further philosophical advance, the speaker
insists that the dead man's goodness penetrated not only
her heart, where it maintains its transformative power, but
those of others as well:

Earth hath received thine earthly part;
Thine heavenly flame has heavenward flown;
But both still linger in my heart,
Still live, and not in mine alone. (P 143)

If these lines do refer to Weightman, then dead for several
years, I would suggest that they express a more philosophical love – agape rather than eros – for an individual who had
provided an image of Christian love, or caritas, in the world.
    Brontë wrote as much of filial love and maternal love as
she wrote of love between a man and a woman. In her poem
'Dreams', the speaker imagines that she cherishes at her
breast 'An infant's form beloved and fair', but she wakes to
find 'myself unloved, alone'. (P 113) She queries her God:

A heart whence warm affections flow,
Creator, thou hast given to me,
And am I only thus [through dreams] to know
How sweet the joys of love would be? (P 113)

In 'Self-Communion', this same idea recurs as Brontë explores the varied forms of love: 'O love is sweet of every kind!' (P 157). In a now-famous passage, she appears to recall her early intimacy with Emily:

Oh, I have known a wondrous joy
In early friendship's pure delight, –
A genial bliss that could not cloy –
My sun by day, my moon by night. (P 157)

But time has brought changes and a division of interests:

I saw that they were sundered now,
The trees that at the root were one:
They yet might mingle leaf and bough,
But still the stems must stand alone. (P 157)

Love and its possibility recede, visiting the speaker only in dreams:

O vainly might I seek to show
The joys from happy love that flow!
The warmest words are all too cold
The secret transports to unfold
Of simplest word or softest sigh,
Or from the glancing of an eye
To say what rapture beams;
One look that bids our fears depart,
And well assures the trusting heart
It beats not in the world alone –
Such speechless raptures I have known,
But only in my dreams. (P 158)

These words, which appear in Brontë's autobiographical poem, suggest that, with passing years, passionate love became an increasingly remote possibility. What replaces it in the poetic imagination, and perhaps in life as well, is hope.

Hopes of earthly bliss give way to hopes of eternal blessedness. And dreams, a frequent motif in Brontë's poetic canon, serve to image a speaker's hopes.

From the earliest poems, dreams are associated with bliss, the only bliss the speaker knows. For example, 'Night' begins with the stanza:

I love the silent hour of night,
For blissful dreams may then arise,
Revealing to my charmed sight
What may not bless my waking eyes! (P 110)

Another poem, written at approximately the same time, has a despairing note because the bliss is confined to dreams:

O God! if this indeed be all
That life can show to me:
If on my aching brow may fall
No freshening dew from Thee:

If with no brighter sun than this
The lamp of hope may glow,
And I may only *dream* of bliss,
And wake, to weary woe. (P 111)

Hope seems a self-delusion because bliss comes only in one's dreams. In this context, we should recall, too, our discussion above of 'Dreams' and 'Self-Communion', in which the speaker dreams of fulfilled love only to awake to emptiness.

Brontë kept wrestling with the relationship of dreams and hope to her quotidian experience. In the early poems, there lingers a possibility that the dreams are images of what

may be and, therefore, the dreams justify hope. In the later
poems, particularly 'Views of Life' and 'Self-Communion',
the picture darkens, and the experienced speaker suggests
that hope is just another 'dream':

Till wintry blasts foreboding blew
Through leafless trees – and then I knew
That hope was all a dream.
But thus, fond youth, she cheated me,
And she will prove as false to thee,
Though sweet her words may seem. (P 118)

The speaker accepts that hope is an illusory dream, but
we may recall from our earlier discussion that the speaker
concludes 'Views of Life' with an assertion that hope is
valuable *despite* its illusory quality. This step marks a
philosophical advance for Brontë. Hope of earthly bliss
deludes, but in that delusion lies redemption from the
pain of daily existence. And those who have kept 'the
narrow way' can reasonably cast their eyes to heaven
and fix their hopes on that bourne.

'Self-Communion' provides the fullest exposition of this
position. The speaker imagines earthly hope as a rainbow
which gradually fades until 'one streak of paly gold'
gives way to 'a rayless arch of sombre grey' (P 158).
The speaker continues:

So must it fare with all thy race
Who seek in earthly things their joy:
So fading hopes lost hopes shall chase,
Till Disappointment all destroy. (P 159)

The answer to disillusionment lies in heavenly hope, imaged
as the sun:

But they that fix their hopes on high

Shall, in the blue refulgent sky,
The sun's transcendent light,
Behold a purer, deeper glow
Than these uncertain gleams shall show,
However fair or bright. (P 159)

The power of the sun, reflected even by the moon at night,
vastly exceeds that of the rainbow, which is evanescent,
however beautiful.

Thus, the later poems finally fix on eternal blessedness
as the proper object of hope; at the same time they
identify heaven as the final home. This emphasis on a
heavenly home culminates yet another ramifying theme in
Brontë's poems, beginning in the earliest Gondal poems.
Throughout the corpus, characters and personas express
an anguished longing for home, first a physically familiar and intimate place, inhabited by loving companions.
Brontë's first poem, 'Verses by Lady Geralda', announces

Father! thou hast long been dead,
    Mother! thou art gone,
Brother! thou art far away,
    And I am left alone. (P 51)

Lady Geralda thus resolves to roam through the world
because,

From such a hopeless home to part
    Is happiness to me,
For nought can charm my weary heart
    Except activity. (P 51)

In the next poem, Zenobia returns to her 'native land' even
though she must leave her love.

When Anne Brontë herself left Haworth for Thorp
Green, she wrote a poem of longing for her home. The
concluding stanza sounds a new note:

But if the sunny summer time
And woods and meadows in their prime
   Are sweet to them that roam –
Far sweeter is the winter bare
With long dark nights and landscape drear
   To them that are at home! (P 80)

Obviously, the physical environment – 'long dark nights
and landscape drear' – is not loveable in itself. This speaker
longs for home as a place of spiritual comfort and solace,
what Brontë's speaker in 'The Consolation' calls 'A home
where heart and soul may rest' (P 94). Or, echoing these
lines in 'Self-Communion', 'a home/Where heart and soul
may kindly rest/Weary and lorn no more to roam' (P 158).

This same emphasis on home as a place of spiritual
repose informs Brontë's poem entitled 'Home'. This lovely
lyric uses alliteration and assonance to capture the contrast
between two different landscapes. The speaker feels the
summons of a physically bleak landscape:

But give me back my barren hills
   Where colder breezes rise:
Where scarce the scattered, stunted trees
   Can yield an answering swell,
But where a wilderness of heath
   Returns the sound as well. (P 100)

She contrasts this landscape to the physically lush place she
inhabits and then asks to be restored to the comparatively
bleak setting:

For yonder garden, fair and wide,

> With groves of evergreen,
> Long winding walks, and borders trim,
>     And velvet lawns between
>
> Restore to me that little spot,
>     With grey walls compassed round,
> Where knotted grass neglected lies,
>     And weeds usurp the ground.
>
> Though all around this mansion high
>     Invites the foot to roam,
> And though its halls are fair within –
>     Oh, give me back my home! (P 100)

In the manuscript, Anne Brontë capitalised her entire last word: HOME. It is worth noting that this poem succeeds partly because of Brontë's fine ability here to image her abstract state in concrete images (something her poetry doesn't always do well). Brontë has captured in imagery of a cultivated garden a material luxury which seems to conceal a spiritual bankruptcy, and she contrasts it to images of a neglected plot disdainful of worldly appearances – where weeds *usurp* the ground – that allows for the cultivation of spiritual riches. Home is now a context for spiritual repose.

In setting up her lyric 'Home,' Brontë is playing on the coded opposition between garden and wilderness which also appears in the other Brontës. For example, Emily's novel sets up this opposition between Thrushcross Grange and Wuthering Heights, and Charlotte Brontë employs it in her letter criticising *Pride and Prejudice*. All are participating in the 'pathos of the picturesque'.[4]

It is interesting that in each of the four of the five poems we have cited above Anne Brontë rhymes 'roam' with 'home'. It seems no accident, for her imagination, like Emily's, fastened on the idea of the orphan and the outlaw: both individuals without homes who are forced

to roam the world. When Anne returned to Haworth in
the summer of 1845, after resigning her post at Thorp
Green, dismayed by Branwell's behaviour in both places,
she wrote two poems emphasising outlaws. The speaker
in poem #43, 'Song', asserts, 'We long have known
and learnt to bear/The wandering outlaw's toil and care'
(P 121). Poem #44, also entitled 'Song', sings of triumph,
'The Tyrants are o'erthrown; the Land is free!' (P 121), yet
the speaker longs 'for the wandering Outlaw's life again!':

With limbs unfettered, conscience undefiled,
And choosing where to wander, where to rest!
Hunted, oppressed, but ever strong to cope –
With toils, and perils – ever full of hope! (P 122)

It seems likely that Anne did not find the spiritual repose
of home in the Haworth of 1845: the speaker of #44
ironically asks: 'Is *this* the end we struggled to obtain?'
Thus, she images herself as an outlaw.

Increasingly, then, 'home' came to mean a place of eternal
rest. In her poem 'To Cowper', Brontë celebrates that
other poet's deserved rest: '. . . and now from earth/Thy
gentle soul is passed./And in the bosom of its God/Has
found its Home at last' (P 84). Similarly, in 'The Three
Guides', the speaker chooses to follow the dictates of the
Spirit of Faith because:

Even above the tempest's swell,
I hear thy voice of love.
Of hope and peace I hear thee tell,
And that blest home above. (P 150)

This final home is invulnerable to the vicissitudes that
render our earthly homes precarious.

## II

We have not yet spoken much of Anne's religious poems and hymns, which constitute a distinctive group. She tended to write such verse on Sundays[5] and, curiously, as if the physical distinction mirrors an imaginative distinction, this group has some significant thematic differences from the others. At the same time, we should admit immediately that we can make no simple distinction between religious poems and the others because Brontë's religious beliefs infused all her work. Nonetheless, there is a body of work, which we shall examine now, that calls on God for sustenance and that seeks to penetrate the will of God. It is this group of poems, no doubt, that Charlotte had in mind when she characterised Anne's verse as 'mournful' and her sister as 'morbid', 'dejected', possessed by 'a tinge of religious melancholy'.[6]

But Charlotte appears, as we have said before, to misread her youngest sister. Where she finds melancholy and morbidity, perhaps projecting her own religious uncertainties onto Anne, we find evidence of a bracing spiritual struggle to obtain divine truths. Three convictions animate the corpus of religious verse. First, God is a loving, not a vengeful, God, and He offers succour to those in need. Second, there exists no external damnation and, however humble or corrupt the petitioner, pardon is sure. These two convictions are obviously related. And third, life is to be cherished as a gift of the Creator.

We may address the first two points by examining the representation of the Creator in Anne's poems. Here we find the New Testament rather than the Old Testament God, the God imaged in Christ, a forgiving God rather than a wrathful God. The poem 'In Memory of a Happy Day in February' describes a personal and loving God so that the speaker 'did not tremble at this power,/I felt that God was mine'. She longs to 'see the glories of his face/Without the veil between' (P 83). In this poem,

too, the perception of God as loving leads naturally to
our second point, the certainty of redemption:

> I knew that my Redeemer lived,
>    I did not fear to die;
> I felt that I should rise again
>    To immortality. (P 83)

Brontë echoes the language of the prayer book to enhance
the power of this lyric.

The loving God is again imaged in Brontë's poem 'To
Cowper', which is interesting for he was haunted by the
sense that he was non-elect – a castaway. I noted in the
previous chapter the extent to which Anne was influenced
by this earlier poet whom she celebrates here as 'Celestial
Bard'. Her identification with him is fervently expressed:

> The language of my inmost heart
>    I traced in every line –
> *My* sins, *my* sorrows, hopes and fears
>    Were there, and only mine. (P 84)

And in Cowper's death and certain resurrection – 'now from
earth/Thy gentle soul is passed./And in the bosom of its
God/Has found its Home at last' – Brontë finds evidence that
'God is love/And answers fervent prayer'. And the speaker
is certain that not only is God loving, but He has provided
succour throughout: 'In thine hours of deepest woe/Thy
God was still with thee' (P 84). The poem, however, does
not conclude on a note of complacency. The speaker finally
considers the alternative to Cowper's resurrection and asks:

> Yet should thy darkest fears be true,
>    If Heaven be so severe

That such a soul as thine is lost,
    O! how shall I appear? (P 85)

No doubt in lines like these Charlotte heard religious 'melancholy', yet to someone like Anne, involved in a continual spiritual self-examination, we may find rather a recognition that certain knowledge is impossible and faith, therefore, imperative, along with a further recognition that she is mortal and fallible and must therefore rely on God's mercy.

In 'Despondency', written a year earlier, the speaker confesses to this fallibility:

And yet, alas! how many times
    My feet have gone astray,
How oft have I forgot my God,
    How greatly fallen away! (P 81)

Despite her recognition of sinfulness, however, she knows she may still petition her Creator and need not despair:

I cannot weep but I can pray,
    Then let me not despair;
Lord Jesus, save me lest I die,
    And hear a wretch's prayer. (P 81)

Not only does Brontë insist here on the certainty of heavenly help, but that certainty informs her poems throughout and always at points of deepest struggle. She is never bereft. In 'A Hymn' of September 10, 1843, the speaker calls herself a 'lost sinner' and asks for faith yet admits:

Without some glimmering in my heart,
I could not raise this fervent prayer;
But O a stronger light impart,
And in thy mercy fix it there! (P 91)

She petitions for release from doubt but finally shifts
the ground of her argument from her own fallibility, as
she does earlier, to her belief in God's son:

If I believe that Jesus died
And waking rose to reign above,
Then surely sorrow, sin and pride
Must yield to peace and hope and love. (P 92)

This ultimate confidence in God's love and help, and a
conviction of redemption through Christ, animate Brontë's
religious poems.

In this context of belief, it is wrong to read struggle
as 'melancholy', and a sense of personal sinfulness as
'morbidity', as Charlotte does. The starting point for
belief is a conviction of one's waverings and unworthiness;
therefore, God is great:

My God! O let me call Thee mine!
Weak wretched sinner though I be,
My trembling soul would fain be Thine,
My feeble faith still clings to Thee. (P 105)

The conclusion here and elsewhere stresses the infinite
mercy of heaven.

The pattern is so insistent that Charlotte seems almost
willfully to have missed it. In 'Fluctuations', the speaker
images God as a sun whose light is reflected in the moon.
She argues that with the departure of the sun, 'The blessed
moon arose on high' to save her 'from despair'. Even as the
night grows darker and drearier, like her spirit, and seems
to eclipse the light, still the moon penetrates the gloom:

Kind Heaven, increase that silvery gleam
        And bid these clouds depart;
And let her kind and holy beam

Restore my fainting heart. (P 104)

The poem 'Confidence' speaks of a similar bleakness: 'Oppressed with sin and woe,/A burdened heart I bear' yet concludes with a now familiar assurance:

In my Redeemer's name,
I give myself to Thee;
And all unworthy as I am
My God will cherish me.

O make me wholly Thine!
Thy love to me impart,
And let Thy holy spirit shine
For ever on my heart! (P 114)

This last stanza, with its assurance of God's love and the speaker's own redemption, was omitted by Charlotte when she printed the poem in 1850. We can only speculate on the reasons for the older sister's editing, but other emendations suggest that Charlotte herself was creating in the verse the Anne whom she called 'morbid'.[7] For example, in 'A Prayer' Charlotte changed 'Unless Thou hasten to relieve,/I know my heart will fall away' to 'Unless Thou hasten to relieve,/Thy supplicant is a castaway' (P 105). The idea of 'castaway' comes, of course, from Cowper's poem of that title, but Anne never endorses the concept in her verse. 'My heart will fall away' – Anne's line – acknowledges the inevitability of doubt, but always as a prelude to God's restoration of faith. Anne's verse expresses intellectual struggle; Charlotte's emendation suggests emotional despair because one fears damnation. Anne's poem 'A Word to the Calvinists' argues against the notion of individual reprobation and election and for the idea of universal salvation, an idea which she cherished and which we shall find fervently defended by the protagonist of *The*

*Tenant of Wildfell Hall*. In this poem, the speaker chastises the complacency of the supposedly elect who can enjoy the prospect of their own undeserved election and the damnation of others. She pinpoints the arrogance of such belief:

And wherefore should your hearts more grateful prove
Because for *all* the Saviour did not die?
Is yours the God of justice and of love
And are your bosoms warm with charity? (P 89)

And the cornerstone of her rebuttal that all are capable of redemption lies in the simple fact we have seen expressed before, 'that none *deserve* eternal bliss I know'. And if no one is deserving of that bliss – 'Unmerited the grace in mercy given' – then any may be redeemed. The difference is of degree and not of kind.

Anne Brontë expresses a generous Christian sensibility that looks first to its own culpability and does not seek to judge others. As a result, her religious poetry avoids didacticism; it concentrates on self-knowledge and self-searching. It eschews prescription and condemnation. Its hallmark might be the words from 'Self-Communion': 'And my worst enemies, I know/Are those within my breast' (P 160).

In Brontë's final poem we find expressed explicitly our third emphasis of the religious poems: the fact that life is sacred and to be cherished. A casual reading of earlier poems may suggest that life on earth is only to be endured until one can claim the heavenly reward. But the entire poetic canon is instinct with life and a conviction that one's feelings, beliefs, and actions matter here on earth, not merely as tokens one can cash in at the gates to the Celestial City. The last poem focuses the tenacity with which Brontë clings to life. As she contemplated death, Brontë wrote these three final stanzas:

Thus let me serve Thee from my heart
Whatever be my written fate,

Whether thus early to depart
Or yet awhile to wait

If Thou shouldst bring me back to life
More humbled I should be;
More wise, more strengthened for the strife,
More apt to lean on Thee.

Should Death be standing at the gate
Thus should I keep my vow;
But, Lord, whate'er my future fate
So let me serve Thee now. (P 164)

Unlike Emily, who appears to have abetted the forces
of death, Anne struggled to retain her hold on life. She
will accept death if inevitable but she will not hasten
its arrival; her reluctance does not stem from doubt of
redemption, rather from a conviction of the value of
life with all its difficulty. In 'The Narrow Way', her
penultimate poem, Brontë finds a telling metaphor for her
own belief: 'But he, that dares not grasp the thorn/Should
never crave the rose' (P 161).

## III

I noted in introducing this chapter that critics have tradi-
tionally divided Anne Brontë's verse between Gondal and
non-Gondal poems and then subdivided the latter category.
I decided not to pursue that familiar organisation so that
we might discover the continuity within her poetic canon
and observe the increasing intellectual sophistication with
which Anne handled her subjects. In that discussion I
have suggested an advancing technical mastery as well,
but in these concluding pages I would like to focus
on questions of diction, image, rhyme, and rhythm to

demonstrate more fully the poetic promise Anne possessed when she died at age twenty-nine.

Charlotte initially commented that Anne's poems had 'a sweet and sincere pathos of their own' (LL II 79), and commentators have followed her in praising the poems' sincerity and authenticity. This quality of 'sincerity' seems to suggest four things about the verse: (1) a relatively simple, non-Latinate diction and a tendency to achieve effects by repetition of those words; (2) simple images with relatively little allusion and few difficult or complex metaphors; (3) a preference for simple, often-repeated rhymes and for metres taken from ballads and hymns; and (4) as a consequence of the foregoing, a felt identity between the poet and speaker. Although the poetry's strength lies in the felt sincerity or authenticity, we should not be so naive as to assume that, therefore, the verse is not carefully crafted. The sincerity is an *effect* of craft in the management of the poetic elements.

While we cannot do an extensive analysis of diction, it is instructive to look at 'Self-Communion' – Anne's autobiographical poem that seems to reconcile 'instinct' or feeling and reason, youth and experience – to examine the operation of one word there: 'toil'. The word expresses both physical difficulty and mental travail. The poem opens with an invocation to 'cease/Thy anxious toil' (P 152). As the speaker recollects the past, she sees a child who 'gropes and toils alone' (P 154) who experiences 'such darkly toiling misery' (P 155). This picture leads to the lesson that 'time, and toil, and truth/An inward hardness can impart' (P 155) ultimately replaced by a hope that 'all our toil be not in vain' (P 157). The word's presence intensifies in the poem's last thirty lines when the speaker recognises that 'it is hard to toil for aye, – /Through sultry noon and twilight grey/To toil and never rest', but accepts that,

With such a glorious hope in view,
I'll gladly toil and suffer too,

Rest *without* toil I would not ask:
I would not shun the hardest task;
Toil is my glory – Grief my gain,
If God's approval they obtain. (P 160)

The word 'toil' becomes a leitmotif in the poem, by its
repetition communicating to us changes both subtle and
substantive in the speaker's consciousness as she accepts the
dictates of reason and experience over the longings of youth.

The same technique works powerfully in Brontë's last
poem where the poet uses the word 'fix'. The speaker
acknowledges, 'But Thou hast fixed another part [death],/
And Thou hast fixed it well' (P 163), a fate to be
accepted only when the speaker 'can fix my heart on
Thee' (P 164). The word means first 'determined', then
'set' or 'riveted', and finally 'attach'. As the single word's
connotations shift, it enhances our perception of process.
The poetry as a whole is always focused on process rather
than on local effects. Its power, then, is cumulative and
rarely to be located in a specific phrase.

The same is true of images. Again in 'Self-Communion'
we can locate one of Anne Brontë's favourite images,
the narrow way, taken from the Bible, 'Wide is the
gate and broad is the way that leadeth to destruction.
Strait is the gate and narrow is the way which leadeth
unto life' (Matthew 7, 13–14). The image appears early
in the poem as the child blindly 'strives to find the
narrow way' (P 154). Her struggles will cease with the
assurance in her Saviour's words: 'I know thy patience
and thy love;/How thou has held the narrow way' (P 160).
The repetition serves to remind us of the spiritual odyssey.

Other images Brontë introduces are less allusive, more
concrete representations of her spiritual state. For example, to capture the withering of love without response,
Brontë writes 'That fires unfed must fall away,/Long
droughts can dry the softest clay' (P 156). Or we will

recall from our discussion of the captive that Brontë effectively images emotional corruption and confinement with 'The bitter cup – the binding chain' (P 159).

The rhymes of 'Self-Communion' also work by employing familiar diction and repetition. The poem employs as rhymes the words 'tears', 'fears', and 'years' a total of ten times. Also common are the rhymes 'grief' and 'relief', 'youth' and 'truth', and 'joy' and 'destroy'. We note that the rhyming words are often opposing in meaning, and in their simplicity and directness they support the dialectical exposition of the poem as it negotiates between the hopes of youth and the truths of experience. Although not repeated, such rhymes as 'prime' and 'time', 'breath' and 'death', 'despair' and 'care', 'grieve' and 'believe' – to name a few – work both locally and cumulatively to underscore the thematic dialectic.[8]

Finally, metre contributes to the entire effect both by its simplicity and its variation. Brontë seemed to have had an ear for the music of verse, and she naturally adopted a variety of metres from hymns to her poems. Perhaps because of her love of hymns and ballads, she seems to favour the iambic tetrameter line. Although the Romantic poets employed iambic pentameter in their great meditative stanzas, Brontë does not and reserves that metre primarily for argument, as in her 'A Word to the Calvinists'. Yet even there, when the speaker switches from expostulation against the Calvinists to matters of her own belief, she adopts a popular hymn metre: alternating iambic tetrameter and iambic trimeter lines. It seems that Brontë found these metres more conducive to self-reflection and revelation. In 'Self-Communion', therefore, Brontë employs predominantly iambic tetrameter lines:

The mist is resting on the hill;
The smoke is hanging in the air;
The very clouds are standing still;

A breathless calm broods everywhere. (P 152)

This metre is the more remarkable because it seems almost
certain that Brontë, as she composed these lines, must have
heard echoes of Wordsworth:

All bright and glittering in the smokeless air.
Never did sun more beautifully steep
In his first splendour, valley, rock, or hill;
Ne'er saw I, never felt, a calm so deep!
The river glideth at his own sweet will:
Dear God! the very houses seem asleep;
And all that mighty heart is lying still!
(Composed upon Westminster Bridge, 11 8–14)

and

It is a beauteous evening, calm and free,
The holy time is quiet as a Nun
Breathless with adoration; the broad sun
Is sinking down in its tranquility;
The gentleness of heaven broods o'er the Sea:
(It is a Beauteous Evening, 11 1–5)

But Wordsworth's lines – iambic pentameter – are beautifully translated by Brontë into the metre she prefers for
spiritual and emotional discovery.

In 'Self-Communion', that iambic tetrameter line works
to advance the poetic argument punctuated at irregular
intervals by iambic trimeter lines that arrest the narrative
progress with a moment of insight or discovery. When the
poem opens, the speaker is counselled to rest and responds:

I would, but Time keeps working still
And moving on for good or ill:
*He* will not rest nor stay.

In pain or ease, in smiles or tears,
He still keeps adding to my years
And stealing life away. (P 152).

The third and sixth lines above, by a shift in metre,
emphasise the inevitable movement of Time, which the next
two such lines also accentuate: 'He steals away my prime!'
and 'The Wasting power of time'. Each subsequent section
of the poem highlights its central idea in these shorter
lines, of which I will give only one example: the picture
of the child – 'How can it stand alone?' – the turning to
God – 'But *God* will not despise!' – the wasting power of
experience – 'And cold will cold beget' – the longing for
love which remains illusory – 'But only in my dreams' –
the resolution to fight foes within and without – 'To combat
and subdue' – and the final recognition that there is rest
beyond the grave – 'However far away!' So the metre moves
with a resistless force to each moment of understanding
and acceptance imitating the imaginative autobiography.
The final rest to the poem and to the life's story finds
expression in the poem's last line, the one iambic pentameter line, which conveys both measure and deliberation:

Press forward, then, without complaint;
Labour and love – and such shall be thy meed. (P 160)

It is a fitting conclusion to a fine poem.

There is, of course, much more to be said about the poetic
resources revealed in Anne Brontë's verse, but enough has
been said to indicate that she showed both power and the
ability to grow as a poet. Had she lived, she might yet
have written poems of real distinction and greatness. As
it is, she produced a moving body of verse, important
in its own right as well as for its insights into her thought.

What is more remarkable is that Anne Brontë was
talented not only as a poet but as a novelist as well;

it is unusual to find writers successful at both although Anne was joined in her achievement by her 'twin', Emily. Anne Brontë's sensibility, like Emily's, uniquely suited her to both genres. But while Emily produced one brilliant novel and them, apparently, wrote no more, Anne was still developing as a novelist when she met her untimely death. And the same artistic growth that we witnessed in the poetry is present in *Agnes Grey* and *The Tenant of Wildfell Hall*, which we shall consider now.

# 4 Agnes Grey: 'all true histories contain instruction'

*Agnes Grey* tells a story of female development. What makes it distinctive from previous novels by women with female protagonists is that Agnes more closely follows a male pattern of development. The classic starting point for the male *Bildungsroman*, or novel of development, is the protagonist's dissatisfaction with home and a corollary desire to gain experience in the larger world. While Agnes cannot simply take to the open road like a male hero, she nonetheless longs 'to see a little more of the world' (AG 4). She resists being kept the '*child* and the pet of the family . . . too helpless and dependent – too unfit for buffeting with the cares and turmoils of life' (AG 4). She wants 'To go out into the world; to enter upon a new life; to act for myself; to exercise my unused faculties; to try my unknown powers; to earn my own maintenance . . .' (AG 10). Anne's sounding of these aims heralds the arrival of a heroine new to fiction, one to whom, as we have seen, Charlotte owes a major debt. Jane Eyre's famous call for general equality has some of Agnes Grey in it: 'Women are supposed to be very calm generally: but women feel just as men feel; they need exercise for their faculites and a field for their efforts as much as their brothers do'.[1] But where Jane Eyre quickly finds her restlessness appeased by the arrival of Rochester, Agnes actually seeks that field for her efforts and exercise for her faculites.

The novel apparently had its origins in Anne Brontë's own experiences as governess first with the Inghams of Blake Hall and then with the Robinsons of Thorp Green. When Anne returned to Thorp Green in the new year of 1842, she began a story called 'Passages in the Life of an Individual'.[2] This work details her own experiences in her two posts and may or may not be a source for her first novel. But even if Anne mined her personal experiences for *Agnes Grey*, we should not confuse Agnes with Anne or neglect to appreciate the high level of artistic shaping present in the published novel. Three years and increasing literary sophistication wrought their effects. Too often, *Agnes Grey* has been read primarily to learn about Anne. Our goal here is to read it as the exquisite novel that George Moore praised in *Conversations in Ebury Street*.

# I

*Agnes Grey* is foremost a novel dealing with education; it is a novel *of* education (Agnes's) and *about* education (her attempts as governess to educate her charges) whose goal is to bring about an education in the reader. Thus, Brontë opens her novel with the claim: 'All true histories contain instruction' (AG 3). There is, as a result, a constantly informing reciprocity of subject and form. For even as Agnes makes only slight gains with her recalcitrant students, she is continually taking home the lessons to herself, learning from the experience, and emerging more fully and forcibly as a self-determining individual. And in the process of displaying her own education, she brings the reader new knowledge.

Because Agnes is a female protagonist seeking to become
educated and knowledgeable about the world, she is distinctive in the nineteenth-century novel. Although Anne Brontë
seems to have been largely oblivious of any feminist or
ideological agenda, her commitment to women's activity and
influence in the world and her suspicion of men as providers
led her to promulgate a feminist thesis: that women must
look to their self-provision. Indeed, if *Agnes Grey* takes
any stance, it is that the novel should both entertain and
instruct, combine the *dulce* with the *utile*. This attitude, as
we have seen, she learned from the eighteenth-century masters. Yet even as Anne Brontë intends that her novel should
instruct, she rigorously insists that the only valid instruction
comes from an unswerving commitment to the representation of 'truth'. Because all meaning derives from her representing reality as she saw it, her work remains strongly novelistic and does not become didactic. Anne Brontë focuses,
then, on representing as fully as possible the quotidian
details of Agnes Grey's employment as governess, and
she lets any instruction emerge from that representation.

Agnes's progression from the Bloomfields' to the
Murrays', from young charges between the ages of four
and seven, to charges between the ages of fourteen and
seventeen, marks her own self-progress and shapes the
reader's developing understanding. When she arrives at
the Bloomfields', Agnes is but a child herself, as she
admits, having been spoiled and pampered by her family.
But Agnes is naive only in experience; in principles and
understanding she is mature. This maturity makes even
more dramatic the disparity between the 'pampered'
and 'indulged' Agnes and the pampered and indulged
Bloomfields. Basically, Agnes has been indulged only
in being overly protected. In contrast, the Bloomfield
children are fairly sophisticated in the ways of the
world and have even learned to manipulate their world
quite cleverly. The indulgence they have been allowed in

the unbridled exercise of their passions, has resulted in an early corruption of their principles.

It is immediately clear to the reader that, in this contest between governess and pupils, the pupils will quickly gain the upper hand precisely because they have neither internal nor external bridles while Agnes knows both the self-restraint taught her by her principles and the external restraints imposed on her as the Bloomfields' 'servant'. Let us address the latter point first. Agnes is clearly instructed that she is not to punish the children. She recognises immediately that 'I had no rewards to offer; and as for punishments, I was given to understand, the parents reserved that privilege themselves; and yet they expected me to keep my pupils in order. Other children might be guided by the fear of anger, and the desire of approbation; but neither the one nor the other had any effect upon these' (AG 22). In an eloquent passage, Agnes sets out the plight of the governess:

I returned, however, with unabated vigour to my work – a more arduous task than any one can imagine, who has not felt something like the misery of being charged with the care and direction of a set of mischievous turbulent rebels, whom his utmost exertions cannot bind to their duty; while, at the same time, he is responsible for their conduct to a higher power, who exacts from him what cannot be achieved without the aid of the superior's more potent authority: which, either from indolence, or the fear of becoming unpopular with the said rebellious gang, the latter refuses to give. I can conceive few situations more harassing than that wherein, however you may long for success, however you may labour to fulfil your duty, your efforts are baffled and set at nought by those beneath you, and unjustly censured and misjudged by those above. (AG 29)

Through Agnes Grey, Anne Brontë has pinpointed what makes the situation of the governess intolerable: entire responsibility for those she cannot bend to her will.

This situation becomes the condition for Agnes's achievement and our evaluation of that achievement. Agnes will serve in two posts, the first of which will challenge her physically, the other spiritually. In both posts, huge demands will be made on her energies, yet she will be given little authority to fulfill those demands. Her success will be measured by her imaginative and flexible adjustment to the limitations imposed on her.

A schoolmistress, in contrast to a governess, has remarkable freedoms. When Agnes joins her mother to open a school, she remarks the difference between the life of a schoolmistress and the life of a governess:

> I set myself with befitting energy to discharge the duties of this new mode of life. I call it *new*, for there was, indeed a considerable difference between working with my mother in a school of our own, and working as a hireling among strangers, despised and trampled upon by old and young. (AG 134)

It is interesting to compare Anne's representations of the governess's life with Charlotte's. Charlotte never succeeded in her posts as governess in a private home, yet, surprisingly, her novels fail to represent the difficulties and humiliations in that position. In *Jane Eyre*, the eponymous heroine finds herself in charge of a docile, if vain, child and in the presence of a motherly housekeeper. The task of teaching her charge scarcely consumes her time, and she has huge tracts of leisure for dalliance with Rochester. It is a highly romanticised portrait of the governess's life.

Agnes Grey, in contrast, finds her job as governess endless and exhausting. She rarely sees her employer, Mr

Bloomfield, and he speaks to her only when exasperated with her failure to control the children. She must do continual battle with recalcitrant and tyrannical pupils. The young master of the family, Tom, amuses himself by 'pulling off [the] legs and wings, and heads of young sparrows' (AG 18). To prevent another such episode of torture, Agnes herself drops a heavy stone and crushes a nest of fledglings that Tom has secured. When thwarted in his pleasures, he becomes violent and frenzied and Agnes's 'only resource was to throw him on his back, and hold his hands and feet till the frenzy was somewhat abated' (AG 22). Mary Ann, the oldest daughter, alternates between rolling on the floor in passive obstinacy or emitting 'shrill, piercing screams, that went through [Agnes's] head like a knife' (AG 25). When the younger Fanny joins her siblings, Agnes finds herself now with a creature of 'falsehood and deception, young as she was, and alarmingly fond of exercising her two favourite weapons of offence and defence; that of spitting in the faces of those who incurred her displeasure, and bellowing like a bull when her unreasonable desires were not gratified' (AG 27).

Despite her early recognition that her situation is untenable, Agnes has no choice but to behave as if she is dealing with students as susceptible as herself. As a result she is continually forced to confess her own failure: 'With me, at her age, or under, neglect and disgrace were the most dreadful of punishments; but on her they made no impression' (AG 25). Her early admission to Mrs Bloomfield that 'I am sorry to say, they [the pupils] have quite deteriorated of late' (AG 27) sets the stage for her dismissal after only six months, a dismissal which her mistress attributes to a 'want of sufficient firmness, and diligent, persevering care on [Agnes's] part' (AG 41).

Her second position, with the Murrays at Horton Lodge, secures her older pupils, less physically demanding but more intellectually demanding. Agnes never loses this position, but the threat of an arbitrary dismissal always hangs over her. Mrs Murray seems to echo Mrs Bloomfield in chastising Agnes: 'I have no desire to part with you, as I am sure you would do very well if you will only think of these things and try to exert yourself a *little* more: then, I am convinced, you would *soon* acquire that delicate tact which alone is wanting to give you a proper influence over the mind of your pupil' (AG 122). We have moved from 'sufficient firmness . . . and persevering care' to 'delicate tact'.

On one level, nothing has changed: Agnes is still expected to compensate for the parents' unacknowledged deficiencies in childrearing. On another level, there are substantial changes: something much more subtle is now demanded of Agnes.

If the Bloomfields initiate her education, acquaintance with the Murrays refines it. She begins with four pupils, but the two boys are quickly dispatched to school. Rosalie, sixteen years, and Matilda, fourteen years, remain, and to these, Agnes is sufficiently close in age that she might seem a sister rather than a governess. Nevertheless, there is never any confusion on that score, because of both rank and character. Agnes's inferiority in the former and her superiority in the latter keep her from intimacy with the Murray sisters. Yet it is important to note that Agnes's superiority of character helps breach the social distance. Agnes remarks of Rosalie, 'And yet, upon the whole, I believe she respected me more than she herself was aware of; because I was the only person in the house who steadily professed good principles, habitually spoke the truth, and generally endeavoured to make inclination bow to duty . . .' (AG 52). Rosalie is possessed of a good temper, 'but from constant indulgence and habitual scorn of reason, she was often testy and capricious; her mind had never been cultivated' (AG 52). Matilda has high animal spirits – 'full of life, vigour, and activity' – but 'as an intelligent being, she was barbarously ignorant, indocile, careless, and irrational' (AG 54).

As at the Bloomfields, Agnes is severely limited in her authority. She is immediately instructed by Mrs Murray that 'when any of the young people do anything improper, if persuasion and gentle remonstrance will not do, let one of the others come and tell me; for I can speak to them more plainly than it would be proper for you to do' (AG 51).

Whereas the Bloomfields needed simple discipline before instruction could begin, the Murrays are sufficiently mature to have acquired some outward restraint and a concern for social reputation. Thus, Agnes can focus on much more subtle points of principle. She observes the sisters' want of discretion, of discrimination, of judgment, of compassion, of generosity. She delineates with precision their rage for attention that leads them to appropriate and use other people for their own amusement. Rosalie and Matilda condescend to the cottagers, treating them as 'stupid and brutish', yet expect the people to 'adore them as angels of light, condescending to minister to their necessities, and enlighten their humble dwellings' (AG 70). Rosalie encourages Mr Hatfield in a flirtation to entertain herself and to have the pleasure of disappointing him. Although engaged to Thomas Ashby, she seeks to snare Mr Weston in her nets before the engagement is publicly announced. Rosalie knows of Ashby's reputation as a reprobate, yet lacks the understanding to have concern for her own future with him. Throughout all, Agnes is anticipating, discriminating, and judging, learning the value of sound principles, individual integrity, and personal independence.

Although Agnes does not confront active and intentional evil at the Murrays, she finds herself grappling with a more insidious because more subtle and pervasive evil stemming from a confusion of right and wrong. Work at the Bloomfields was physically strenuous; work at the Murrays is morally strenuous. Agnes reveals to the reader that:

Already I seemed to feel my intellect deteriorating, my
heart petrifying, my soul contracting; and I trembled
lest my very moral perceptions should become deadened,
my distinctions of right and wrong confounded, and
all my better faculties be sunk, at last, beneath the
baneful influence of such a mode of life. (AG 80)

This corruption of innocence by the 'baneful influence
of such a mode of life' will become a central theme in
*The Tenant of Wildfell Hall*. Here, the fear is sounded
only at the moment that it is removed: 'Mr Weston rose
at length upon me, appearing like the morning-star in my
horizon, to save me from the fear of utter darkness' (AG
80). In addition, Agnes does not fall prey to the corruption because she imprints her character on the Murray
sisters more than they influence her. She recognises at
one point that they 'became a little less insolent, and
began to show some symptoms of esteem' (AG 58).

Agnes herself gives us the full measure of her achievement by parroting her pupils' own evaluation of her.
Because Brontë filters the Murray sisters' changes of
opinion through Agnes's more generous and discriminating
sensibility, we are able to appreciate two key things: (1)
the respect Agnes has genuinely earned; and (2) Agnes's
subtle and ironic understanding of the limits of that
respect. Agnes summarises her influence in this way:

Miss Grey was a queer creature: she never flattered,
and did not praise them half enough; but whenever she
did speak favourably of them, or anything belonging to
them, they could be quite sure her approbation was
sincere. She was very obliging, quiet, and peaceable
in the main, but there were some things that put her
out of temper: they did not much care for that, to be
sure, but still it was better to keep her in tune; as
when she was in a good humour she would talk to

them, and be very agreeable and amusing sometimes, in her way; which was quite different to mamma's, but still very well for a change. She had her own opinions on every subject, and kept steadily to them – very tiresome opinions they often were; as she was always thinking of what was right and what was wrong, and had a strange reverence for matters connected with religion, and an unaccountable liking for good people. (AG 58–59)

It is a measure of Agnes's own successful education that she has succeeded to the degree she has, especially in view of the limitations put on her powers.

If Agnes is often severely crippled in her efforts to teach her students by the restraints imposed by the Bloomfields and Murrays, she is, in key ways, enabled in these situations by her own self-restraints. She does not complain or lament or indulge in self-pity. She can see beyond the particular situation to her larger goals, and she 'longed to show my friends that, even now, I was competent to undertake the charge and able to acquit myself honourably to the end' (AG 28). Although we may find aspects of Agnes's self-suppression excessive – she says, for example, 'I judged it my wisest plan to subdue every resentful impulse, suppress every sensitive shrinking' (AG 28–29) or 'I sometimes felt myself degraded by the life I led, and ashamed of submitting to so many indignities' (AG 58) – the episodes culminate in self-affirmation rather than self-negation. She is both enabled and emboldened. She may adopt a policy of compliance to her employers, but the fact that it is a policy suggests the measure of control she preserves. She always has the choice of returning to her home; thus, she assesses her situation on the basis of the autonomy she has achieved rather than on the difficulties she encounters. Consequently, although Agnes is like many nineteenth-century heroines in having to turn inward to cultivate her spiritual resources, she differs from those heroines because this mode culminates in increasing mastery of the secular world. Although dismissed from her first post, Agnes chooses to depart from her second to open a school with her mother. The result is a female *Bildungsroman*, or novel of development, that both draws from a tradition of other such novels and departs significantly from it. Cultivation of the spiritual life, leading to mastery of the passions, seems to ensure a greater degree of self-determination for Agnes rather than an increase in self-abnegation typical of the protagonist of the female *Bildungsroman*. All of Agnes's pupils have been tossed about by their passions and, even with maturity, they remain unable to curb their indulgence in whims and their rage for attention. Agnes can see the evils to which they are vulnerable in maturity and, learning to conquer potential weaknesses in her own character, establishes herself as an independent woman.

Brontë's Agnes cannot replicate exactly the pattern of a male protagonist in a *Bildungsroman*. For example, the hero's two love affairs, one sexual and one spiritual, would culminate in social expulsion for a female protagonist. Nonetheless, Brontë uses the physical stresses suffered under the Bloomfields and the spiritual stresses endured under the Murrays as analogues for those other definitive developmental experiences en route to maturity. So Agnes, like the male protagonist, concludes her journey in her achievement of individual autonomy and social authority.

Through teaching, Agnes has plumbed her own strengths and honed her own understanding. She has completed her own education. Anne Brontë has carefully structured the novel to emphasise this completion. We have acknowledged that the novel was, perhaps, autobiographical in its inception, but Brontë shaped her materials towards novelistic ends. Agnes, as narrator, focuses on those episodes in which her education is being forwarded. She passes over her returns to home during the holidays. Her longing for such holidays is strongly represented to ensure our appreciation

of her stoicism, but Brontë does not represent the holidays
themselves because they are not germane to the novel's
subject. Brontë opens Chapter four with Agnes's words,
'I spare my readers the account of my delight on coming
home . . . I returned, however, with unabated vigour to
my work . . .' (AG 29). Later, Agnes comments, 'for I *was*
lonely. Never, from month to month, from year to year,
except during my brief intervals of rest at home, did I
see one creature to whom I could open my heart, or
freely speak thoughts with any hope of sympathy, or even
comprehension' (AG 79). But those precious, brief intervals
do not make their way into the plot. Agnes concludes her
tenure with the Bloomfields remarking, 'vexed, harassed,
disappointed as I had been, and greatly as I had learned
to love and value my home, I was not yet weary of
adventure, nor willing to relax my efforts' (AG 41). Her
several months at home are related in three pages and
primarily establish two central points: Agnes must succeed
in the world, and a woman need not marry to succeed.
Agnes's mother counsels the father, 'But it's no matter
whether [our daughters] get married or not: we can devise
a thousand honest ways of making a livelihood' (AG 42).

## II

Distinctively, the novel is neither male – nor marriage –
oriented. Although it will conclude with wedding bells, that
traditional bourne of eighteenth- and nineteenth-century
novels, the reader is not led to expect marriage as Agnes's
fulfilment. We may contrast what Anne Brontë does with
what Jane Austen does. Both writers are concerned with
the education of their protagonists. We may say that
Austen yokes the heroine's movement toward marriage
with her education; that is, an Austen protagonist must
learn to discern the true from the false, the flashy from

the substantial, the truly amiable man from the merely agreeable one. This is particularly true for Elizabeth Bennet and Emma Woodhouse. Their lessons in discernment culminate in their choice of suitable partners. Agnes's lessons, in contrast, all culminate in her independency. Perhaps this emphasis signals Anne Brontë's very different experiences. The Brontës were much poorer and of a lower class than the Austens; thus Anne had to think constantly about profitable employment while Austen never worked. More important, Anne could never rely on her brother for support as Austen could on hers. As a result, Brontë's feminism ultimately takes on a different character.

Anne Brontë has structured her narrative to emphasise the acquisition of independence. Her heroine meets a suitable man, a clergyman Mr Weston, relatively late in the novel. She first recognises his excellence and then discovers in herself symptoms of a growing attraction. When she leaves him to open a school with her mother, she has made this choice to depart. She has been encouraged to believe he might seek her hand, and, at first she pines for this resolution like a typical heroine. She reveals that:

> I knew my strength was declining, my appetite had failed, and I was grown listless and desponding; – and if, indeed, he could never care for me, and I could never see him more – if I was forbidden to minister to his happiness – forbidden, for ever, to taste the joys of love, to bless and to be blessed – then, life must be a burden, and if my Heavenly Father would call me away, I should be glad to rest. (AG 136)

But no sooner has Agnes reached this pitch than she resolves, "'No, by His help I will arise and address myself diligently to my appointed duty'" (AG 137). The consequence is a rapid restoration of tranquillity of mind and 'bodily health and vigour'.

At this point we may note that there exists many another heroine of spunk who recovers her spirits without a proposal. We may recall Elizabeth Bennet's thoughts when doubtful that Darcy will propose again: 'If he is satisfied with only regretting me, when he might have obtained my affections and hand, I shall soon cease to regret him at all'.[3] But, while Darcy immediately makes his appearance in Austen's novel, Brontë's narrative seems deliberately to shift to another scene and to a new focus: Rosalie's marriage. Agnes is invited by her former pupil to visit her in her splendour as Lady Ashby. What she finds is a woman in misery, yet another reminder that marriage does not necessarily culminate in fulfilment for a woman and, indeed, may mark her further imprisonment. When Agnes returns home, full of a sense of her own riches, she is rejuvenated: 'Refreshed, delighted, invigorated, I walked along, forgetting all my cares, feeling as if I had wings to my feet, and could go at least forty miles without fatigue, and experiencing a sense of exhilaration to which I had been an entire stranger since the days of early youth' (AG 150).

It is only at this point of physical health, mental equanimity, and the personal fulfilment of financial and emotional independence that Mr Weston arrives to propose. The marriage simply stands as a coda to Agnes's journey toward autonomy.

The novel not only proposes that marriage *per se* does not constitute fulfilment, but also, as we have seen in the example of Rosalie, that marriage to the wrong partner might condemn one to a life of unhappiness. I suggested earlier that the novel was neither marriage- nor male-oriented and the two are obviously related. The entire novel presents only one admirable man: Mr Weston. Although he is a good man, he is not at all romanticised. In contrast to Charlotte's heroes and Emily's Heathcliff, he is not stern, commanding, and forceful. He is strong mainly in his commitment to principle and duty. He is somewhat phlegmatic and unemotional, deliberate and precise. Anne seems to avoid any romantic idealisation of men, particularly of men with power and money. In them, she finds large scope for abuse.

The men who employ her, Mr Bloomfield and Mr Murray, are contemptible. Neither man does her the courtesy of introducing himself. She infers their identities from their behaviour. Neither is prepossessing. Mr Bloomfield is a 'man of ordinary stature – rather below than above – and rather thin than stout, apparently between thirty and forty years of age: he had a large mouth, pale, dingy complexion, milky blue eyes, and hair the colour of a hempen cord' (AG 20). Mr Murray is a 'tall, stout gentleman, with scarlet cheeks and crimson nose' whom Agnes often hears 'swearing and blaspheming against the footmen, groom, coachman, or some other hapless dependent' (AG 50). Neither exercises any proper authority over his children. Their deficiencies reveal themselves in the defects of their children.

The most pernicious effect of these careless fathers is the automatic assumption of authority, importance and careless disdain for so-called lesser creatures they bequeath their sons. We will recall that Tom Bloomfield, Agnes's first charge, likes to torture fledglings which his papa says is 'just what *he* used to do when *he* was a boy. Last summer he gave me a nest full of young sparrows, and he saw me pulling off their legs and wings, and heads, and never said anything . . .' (AG 18). But not only birds suffer under this masculine dictatorship. Women do as well. When Agnes protests, 'Surely, Tom, you would not strike your sister! I hope I shall *never* see you do that', he replies, '"You will sometimes: I am obliged to do it now and then to keep her in order"' (AG 16). And this general attitude is fostered in young boys by the men who surround them. Mr Robson, Mrs Bloomfield's brother, 'encouraged Tom's propensity to persecute the lower creation, both by precept and example' (AG 37). He chortles when Tom heaps opprobrious epithets upon Agnes – 'Curse me, if ever I saw a nobler little scoundrel than that.

He's beyond petticoat government already . . .' (AG 39) –
recalling Walpole's characterisation of Mary Wollstonecraft
as a 'hyena in petticoats'. Anne Brontë will explore and
expose more fully this masculine arrogance toward women
in *The Tenant of Wildfell Hall*, but it is evident even here
that the subject concerns her greatly. Here, too, she links,
as she will in *The Tenant*, male drinking, masculinity, and
male tyranny. Mr Robson encourages his nephew 'to believe
that the more wine and spirits he could take, and the
better he liked them, the more he manifested his bold
and manly spirit, and rose superior to his sisters' (AG 37).

In linking women with the 'lower creatures', Anne
Brontë also suggests in this novel that a woman may take
the measure of the man from his treatment of animals.
Mr Hatfield, the vain and arrogant rector in the Murray's
parish, consumed by his flirtation with Rosalie Murray,
kicks a poor lady's cat 'right across th' floor, an' went
after [the Murray girls] as gay as a lark' (AG 74). And he
harasses the poor woman's spirit much as he harasses her
cat's body. Mr Weston, in contrast, 'spake so civil like –
and when th' cat, poor thing, jumped on to his knee, he
only stroked her, and gave a bit of a smile: so I thought
that was a good sign; for once, when she did so to th'
Rector, he knocked her off, like as it might be in scorn
and anger . . .' (AG 75–76). Agnes has formed an affection
for a little terrier at the Murrays' and is heart-broken when
he is taken away and 'delivered over to the tender mercies
of the village rat-catcher, a man notorious for his brutal
treatment of his canine slaves' (AG 118). Mr Weston
heralds his arrival to propose to Agnes with this little canine
messenger, whom he has rescued from the rat-catcher.
Agnes's satisfaction that Snap, the terrier, now 'has a good
master' anticipates her own acceptance of Mr Weston.

It seems that Charlotte may have drawn this mode of
characterisation from her sister. In *Shirley*, the eponymous
character argues that to know if a man is truly good, 'we

watch him, and see him kind to animals, to little children, to poor people'.[4] In praising Robert Moore, Caroline Helstone replies, 'I know somebody to whose knee that black cat loves to climb; against whose shoulder and cheek it likes to purr. The old dog always comes out of his kennel and wags his tail, and whines affectionately when somebody passes'. Charlotte intensifies her similarity to Anne's description in a succeeding passage: 'He quietly strokes the cat, and lets her sit while he conveniently can, and when he must disturb her by rising, he puts her softly down, and never flings her from him roughly'.[5] Louis Moore, too, has his excellence measured by his sympathy with animals. And Shirley's cousin, Henry, is distinguished from the usual school-boy by his behaviour with animals. Shirley reveals, 'Generally, I don't like school-boys: I have a great horror of them. They seem to me little ruffians, who take an unnatural delight in killing and tormenting birds, and insects, and kittens, and whatever is weaker than themselves . . .'[6] Finally, as if recalling *Agnes Grey*, Martin Yorke is reminded at one point 'of what he had once felt when he had heard a blackbird lamenting for her nestlings, which Matthew had crushed with a stone'.[7] Charlotte has learned from Anne a very powerful mode for realistically delineating male tyranny.

Anne deserves recognition for the clarity with which she details men's contempt for women in Victorian society and for the corollary recognition that, given this contempt and the power men hold in marriage, women are likely to suffer in that relationship. In her first position, Agnes witnesses a scene in which Mr Bloomfield berates his wife for her presumed negligence of duties. Agnes relates that, 'I never felt so ashamed and uncomfortable in my life for anything that was not my own fault' (AG 21). When Rosalie Murray marries the reprobate Lord Ashby – described as 'disagreeably red about the eyelids', with 'a general appearance of langour and flatness, relieved by a sinister expression in the mouth and the dull, soulless eyes' – she anticipates that because he adores her, he will 'let [her] have her own way' (AG 146). But she discovers to her chagrin and pain that '*he will* do as he pleases, and I must be a prisoner and a slave'. Rosalie cries out, 'Oh, I would give ten thousand worlds to be Miss Murray again! It is *too* bad to feel life, health, and beauty wasting away, unfelt and unenjoyed, for such a brute as that!' (AG 147). Ironically, Rosalie has earlier glimpsed her impending prison and confided to Agnes, 'But if I could be always young, I would be always single' (AG 64). Less vain than Rosalie and independent of male approval, Agnes is more suspicious of marriage as woman's fulfilment.

Even her parents' own example has given Agnes cause to proceed cautiously and to ensure her own autonomy before committing herself to another. Although Anne Brontë represents Mrs Grey's decision to marry a 'poor parson' as a positive one, one for which Agnes's mother is wholly admirable, Mr Grey is painted less sympathetically. Agnes confides that 'saving was not my father's forte. He would not run in debt (at least, my mother took good care he should not), but while he had money he must spend it' (AG 5). Ultimately Richard Grey decides to speculate with his small capital and loses it. Agnes, her sister, and her mother all survive the shock, but Mr Grey 'was completely overwhelmed by the calamity' (AG 6). Not only does he plunge them into poverty, but, incapable of rising to the challenge himself, he becomes an additional burden on his struggling family. His weakness leaves them vulnerable and ultimately increases their responsibility. In contrast, Mrs Grey is resourceful, energetic, strong, and determined. She ultimately heads a little community of women that provides a much more positive image of relationship than that of heterosexual marriage.

Anne Brontë, however, does not allow this female community to resolve her novel. As I've pointed out above, Agnes ultimately marries. But she does so only after we have been made to feel she has the option of self-support and of a nurturing female community. These are unusual options to find represented in a novel set in Victorian England. And, lest we feel that, after all, Agnes, like many another heroine before her, has succumbed to marriage as the only viable option, we have the positive portrait of successful Mrs Grey, who refuses to live with her daughters, 'saying she could now afford to employ an assistant, and would continue the school till she could purchase an annuity sufficient to maintain her in comfortable lodgings . . .' (AG 157). This might yet be Agnes's fate, and not a bad one, we feel, in a world that encourages male strength to take the form of tyranny and that indulges male weakness.

## III

I've suggested above that the novel's strength lies in its quiet realism. Here, it is well to note what cannot be too often emphasised: Anne Brontë's talent for painting her milieu. She gives us, more accurately than most of her contemporaries, a sense of what Victorian female leisured life was like. She communicates the lassitude, the emptiness, the boredom. She makes us experience the significance of social rank: the disdain in which Agnes is held by the neighbouring gentlemen, the rudeness with which servants – taking a cue from their masters – treat her. We share the frustration of being a servant, subject to the whims of one's masters, whether these whims take the form of either demanding that she finish the tedious parts of pictures and of fancywork or encouraging her to appear unobtrusive when unwanted and infinitely accommodating when needed.

No one has communicated better than Anne Brontë the sheer physical demands of the period. I have already detailed her exhausting struggles with her pupils. Travel, too, is particularly demanding. When Agnes first arrives at the Bloomfields, she has only a minute to try to put herself in order and is dismayed at her appearance: 'The cold wind has swelled and reddened my hands, uncurled and entangled my hair, and dyed my face of a pale purple; add to this my collar was horridly crumpled, my frock splashed with mud, my feet clad in stout new boots' (AG 14). Her second journey is even more difficult. Agnes leaves on a dark winter morning and relates that 'the heavy snow had thrown such impediments in the way of both horses and steam-engines, that it was dark some hours before I reached my journey's end, and that a most bewildering storm came on at last . . . I sat resigned, with the cold, sharp snow drifting through my veil and filling my lap, seeing nothing . . .' (AG 47). Brontë captures, too, Agnes's nausea from being stuffed into a carriage and riding backward, and her humiliation at being forced to dawdle behind a walking party because she is regarded as a 'mere domestic, who knew her own place too well to walk beside such fine ladies and gentlemen . . .' (AG 85).

Because *Agnes Grey* is dedicated to portraying a truth about Victorian life, Brontë eschews dramatic scenes. Many readers will find the 'plot' turgid, so little happens. But that is, as I have argued, because the novel is about education. It intends to keep the reader focused on the life of a mind.

Certain classic themes are generated out of these formal ends. First, the family is the primary focus of education. All subsequent influences cannot wholly eradicate the deficiencies produced by early indulgence and insufficient guidance. But if the understanding has been trained and the passions reigned in, then a great flowering is possible.

A corollary theme suggests that money and a monied, class society lie at the base of this pernicious indulgence. Having been encouraged by their wealth and social position to think well of themselves, the upper classes fail to ground their pride properly in their understanding, judgment,

and discrimination. Anne Brontë makes it evident that
in moving to the Murrays' Horton Lodge, Agnes has
enjoyed an accession of social prestige: 'The house was
a very respectable one; superior to Mr Bloomfield's, both
in age, size, and magnificence' (AG, 56). Mrs Grey has
distinguished the Bloomfields from the Murrays terming
the former 'purse-proud tradespeople and arrogant upstarts'
while the latter are characterised as 'genuine thorough-bred
gentry' (AG 44, 46). However, although the Murray's
outrank the Bloomfields, they share their coarseness and
crudity. There is more superficial polish but no increase
in real elegance. And when Agnes finally visits that star
in the social firmament – Rosalie Murray, now Lady
Ashby – she remarks on departing:

It was with a heavy heart that I bade adieu to poor
Lady Ashby, and left her in her princely home. It was
no slight additional proof of her unhappiness that she
should so cling to the consolation of my presence, and
earnestly desire the company of one whose general tastes
and ideas were so little congenial to her own. (AG 148).

We feel that Agnes, who cannot possibly envy Rosalie
Murray nor desire *her* company, possesses a life both richer
and more meaningful.

Growing out of Brontë's perception that money and
power corrupt, is her recognition that the only real source
of happiness lies in cultivating the spiritual life and pursuing
the dictates of religion. Agnes tells Rosalie, by way of
farewell: 'The best way to enjoy yourself is to do what is
right and hate nobody. The end of Religion is not to teach
us how to die, but how to live; and the earlier you become
wise and good, the more of happiness you secure' (AG 148).
We discover, then, that the religious theme is linked to the
educational theme that controls the novel; religion helps
teach us how to live the good life. It provides the foundation

for moral principle, and it stands as a bulwark against despair. By thoroughly integrating the religious theme with the educational one, Brontë precludes the intrusion of any awkward or disruptive moral didacticism into her tale. When we finish the novel, we must feel that Brontë has accomplished her end of furthering our instruction through her protagonist's. But, perhaps more important, we feel that the process has gone on unobtrusively while we were fully engaged with the quiet story of an unassuming young woman.

And, once more, we are reminded of Brontë's triumph: her ability to take materials superficially so unengaging, so devoid of dramatic incident, and to involve us so deeply in them. Finally, Anne Brontë's achievement in *Agnes Grey* must be measured by her success in transforming a radical theme of women's education and independence into a subject matter so wholly reasonable. Brontë's next novel, to be her last, will demonstrate the as-yet-unexplored reach of her talent and suggest what might have been had she lived.

# 5 The Tenant of Wildfell Hall: 'wholesome truths' versus 'soft nonsense'

In writing *The Tenant of Wildfell Hall*, Anne Brontë achieved a dramatic narrative and philosophical advance from *Agnes Grey*. Although we can trace the continuity in certain themes between the two novels, the manner, style, technique, character, and episode through which those themes are developed and examined differ substantially. There is also a new thematic depth, an increasingly mature handling of theme, and a deepening grasp of the ways in which form and subject interpenetrate. Instead of presenting the quiet story of one individual's growth related through that individual's perspective, Anne Brontë's second novel details the growth or deterioration of several characters and employs a sophisticated technique of layered narratives that undergirds the novel's preeminent theme. This theme presents 'truth' or 'reality' as a complex interpretation, inevitably coloured by individual personalities. It is a product of Brontë's own sophisticated appreciation of context and 'truth'.

# I

In brief, *The Tenant of Wildfell Hall* rewrites the story of the Fallen Woman as a story of female excellence. In so doing, it takes on a radical feminist dimension. The outraged reviews that greeted its publication – the castigations it received for its coarseness and brutality – were no doubt prompted as much by the portrayal of the protagonist as by the portrait of her dissolute first husband. Her decision to flee an unhappy marriage with her young son violated Victorian social convention and law. Caroline Norton, a later advocate for the amendment of those laws, suffered from a situation analogous to that of the protagonist in Brontë's novel. In 1855, seven years after the publication of Brontë's novel, Norton enumerated the injustices, all of which stemmed from the fact that a married woman in England had no legal existence. She had no possessions, 'her property is *his* property', she 'cannot legally claim her own earnings', she 'may not leave her husband's house', he may 'take her by force' from the house of anyone who may 'harbour' her, and she may not divorce her husband 'however profligate he may be'.[1]

We may find surprising the degree to which Anne Brontë's plot in *The Tenant* makes a fictional argument for the correction of these legal imbalances. There, a young and idealistic young woman marries a man whose character is already in need of reformation. Believing herself called to this task, she begins optimistically only to discover that she is powerless to effect any changes that cannot be wrought by the force of moral suasion. She has no social or legal leverage. Ultimately, finding her son and herself sinking into the corruption generated by her husband, she plans to flee, only to be defeated on a first attempt when her husband, discerning her intention, confiscates all of her property. Prompted by her husband's introduction of his mistress into the house as his son's governess, she makes a successful second attempt, but she must carefully guard her identity from her all-too-inquisitive neighbours or she may be betrayed to her husband and forced to return.

These events, at the heart of the novel, are told only retrospectively. The novel is, in fact, doubly retrospective. When it opens in 1847, the narrator, a middle-aged Gilbert Markham, is writing to his friend Halford. He has felt that he owes Halford a return for an earlier confidence and will now make good his debt with an 'old-world story . . . a full and faithful account of certain circumstances connected with the most important event of my life' (TWH 34). Gilbert's narrative itself begins twenty years earlier, in the autumn of 1827, with the arrival of a new tenant at Wildfell Hall. Helen Graham, the mysterious tenant, is that woman who has violated Victorian social convention by leaving her husband, and her story – incorporated later through her diary – begins on June 1, 1821. Thus, the novel progressively probes the past and its meaning – first by twenty years and then by an additional six. Supposedly a young widow, Helen immediately becomes the object of community speculation even as she is the occasion of Gilbert Markham's narrative.

It must be of primary interest for us to ask why Anne Brontë structures her narrative in this way,[2] allowing us to see Helen only through Gilbert's eyes for the first third of the novel, and then presenting us with the long retrospective of Helen's life with her husband, Arthur Huntingdon. Details of the marriage are recounted in Helen's diary beginning, as we have noted, in 1821 and concluding with her arrival at Wildfell Hall in 1827 when Gilbert's narrative commences. Many critics have objected to the artistic infelicity of such a device, particularly to the huge chunk of diary (parts of volumes I and III and all of volume II). George Moore early suggested that Anne Brontë failed here 'not for lack of genius but of experience'. His remedy was to have the heroine 'tell the young farmer her story, and an entrancing scene you will make of the telling . . . The presence of your heroine, her voice, her gestures . . . would preserve the atmosphere of a passionate and original love story'.[3] But what Moore failed to see was that oral 'telling' in this novel would not do.

Anne Brontë has made 'authority' in story-telling a key issue. The oral tale here has a free circulation without accountability whereas the written story has an agent who may be held accountable. The novel is alive with rumour, scandal, conjecture, slander, gossip – various kinds of oral reports – and they are largely discredited or, at least, highly suspect. Because Helen Graham herself is the most frequent subject of such 'free' discourse, we are forced to hold it suspect and more fully credit the written account with all its gestures toward verification. In the preamble to his story, for instance, Gilbert Markham is at pains to justify his version of events and asserts:

> Among the letters and papers I spoke of, there is a certain faded old journal of mine, which I mention by way of assurance that I have not my memory alone – tenacious as it is – to depend upon; in order that your credulity may not be too severely taxed in following me through the minute details of my narrative. (TWH 34)

Gilbert's recounting, then, is an attempt to stop the free flow of oral exchange.

The novel opens with Gilbert's sister, Rose, 'bursting with . . . an important piece of news', that a 'single lady' has let Wildfell Hall, although 'the place is in ruins' (TWH 37). Gilbert's brother, Fergus, remarks that he hopes she is a 'witch' (TWH 38). His joking conjecture anticipates the communal suspicion and predisposition to gossip about the 'mysterious lady' (TWH 39). As Jan Gordon has noted in reference to this novel, such gossip or '"overheard language" has no authorship that can be readily identified. It is a speculative language thrown out at that which is only incompletely understood, and its origins can never be traced or

determined'.[4] Without author and authority, it is endlessly
expansive and difficult to contain. Gilbert reveals that 'During
the next four months . . . the ladies continued to talk
about her' (TWH 72). He admits to Helen that 'we often
hold discussions about you; for some of us have nothing better to do than to talk about our neighbours' concerns' (TWH
83). Gradually the talk takes on the character of 'shocking
reports about Mrs Graham' and Gilbert is troubled by 'what
they were, by whom originated, and on what foundations
raised – and how they could the most effectually be silenced
or disproved' (TWH 96-97). Later in the novel when Gilbert
tries to quell a rumour, he is rebuked, 'Well, I only "tell the
tale as 'twas told to me": I don't vouch for the truth of it;
but at the same time, I don't see what reason Sarah should
have for deceiving me, or her informant for deceiving her'
(TWH 463). Gilbert can label these reports 'the calumnies
of malicious tongues' or 'vile constructions' or 'lying inven-
tions!' or 'malignant, baseless slanders' (TWH 120, 145),
but he cannot contain and suppress them orally. He simply
adds another 'report' to those already in circulation.

It is only by writing, by becoming author and authority,
that he can, in some measure, control the free circulation of
talk by enclosing it in his own overarching interpretation.
This is the goal of his letter to Halford and the function
of his narrative within Brontë's novel, to authorise his
version of events and his interpretation of Helen Graham.

The gossip, or 'talk', is objectionable not only because
it is without identifiable authority, but also because it is
'small'. When Helen complains that 'I was wearied to
death with small talk', Gilbert replies, 'It is that they
think it a *duty* to be continually talking . . . and so never
pause to think' (TWH 103). In *The Tenant of Wildfell Hall*,
gossip is identified with mindlessness, often associated
with women but not exclusively (Reverend Millward feeds
on just such rumours), whereas writing suggests both
thought and authority.

Helen's recourse against such abuses of language is her diary which purports to be a 'full and faithful account' even as Markham's long letter to Halford purports to be such an account. Furthermore, the pretence of the diary – that it is not written for an audience except oneself – makes it even less subject to the charge of self-interest than Gilbert's letter is. True, it will be marked by the bias of the writer, but theoretically it is disinterested in a way that Helen's conversations with Markham can never be. Once she is interested in the young farmer, that interest jeopardises the disinterestedness of her report on her first marriage.

It is only by incorporating Helen's diary into his own narrative that Markham can reinterpret the Fallen Woman and runaway wife of Victorian convention as the model of excellent womanhood that the novel proposes. Helen's diary and her subsequent letters to her brother – also appropriated and incorporated by Markham – constitute primary evidence for the interpretive act, which was initiated by Markham's 'reading' of Helen's face and his conversations with her. He argues: 'Did I not know Mrs Graham? Had I not seen her, conversed with her time after time? Was I not certain that she, in intellect, in purity and elevation of soul, was immeasurably superior to any of her detractors; that she was, in fact, the noblest, the most adorable, of her sex I had ever beheld, or even imagined to exist?' (TWH 101). He asserts: 'I don't know whether I've told you before, but [her eyes] were full of soul, large, clear and nearly black' (TWH 86) Or he claims, 'There is such a thing as looking through a person's eyes into the heart, and learning more of the height, and breadth, and depth of another's soul in one hour, than it might take you a lifetime to discover . . .' (TWH 114).

This evidence of the eye gives way, of course, to the evidence of her diary – a written testimony to her excellence. Her diary validates her even though the community persists in vilifying her. And, more important, it stands to validate her at the very moment that Gilbert begins to doubt her, as he has recently witnessed *with his own eyes* a love scene between Lawrence and Helen. Not knowing that they are brother and sister, he misreads the situation and blames her, claiming that he had no obligation to let her explain because she could not have 'made me discredit the evidence of my senses' (TWH 145). Yet the evidence of his senses, his eyes and ears, is palpably misleading in the absence of full knowledge of context.

To make this point that things are often not what they appear to the senses, Anne Brontë replicates this scene at two other significant points in the novel: first, in Huntingdon's scenes with his wife and mistress in the shrubbery, and second, in Hargrave's attempt to compromise Helen. The first scene offers a striking parallel to the episode Markham witnesses, but, in this case, the partners are culpable. Yet Helen herself has misread the situation at first. When she stumbles upon her husband in the dark and he eagerly embraces her, she does not realise for an entire day, and then only when confronted with Annabella in her husband's arms, that the 'burst of kindness was for his paramour, the start of horror [which succeeded the passion when he recognised Helen] for his wife' (TWH 314). Her first interpretation of these events is that 'the affection is genuine; he is not sick of me yet' (TWH 306).

In the second scene between Hargrave (who is trying to force Helen to elope with him) and Helen, the former is culpable and the latter innocent, yet the scene is misread by Huntingdon's friend Grimsby and by Huntingdon himself until Helen forces Hargrave to interpret its meaning for the others. Hargrave, in a moment of betrayal, realises immediately that he can *use* the situation to secure what all his pleas have not accomplished: the consent of Helen to flee with him. When he sees they have been overheard, 'a gleam of malicious triumph lit up his countenance' (TWH 363). He threatens Helen, 'That is Grimsby . . . He will report what he has seen to Huntingdon . . . He will give such a version of this story as will leave no doubt at all, about your character, in the minds of those who hear it. Your fair fame is gone; and nothing that I or you can say can ever retrieve it' (TWH 363). But Helen, a better hermeneutician than Hargrave, knows that interpretations can be changed. She demands Hargrave's cooperation:

'Tell those gentlemen . . . these *men*, whether or not I yielded to your solicitations.'

'I don't understand you, Mrs Huntingdon.'

'You *do* understand me, sir; and I charge you upon your honour as a gentleman (if you have any), to answer truly. Did I, or did I not?'

'No,' muttered he, turning away.

'Speak up, sir; they can't hear you. Did I grant your request?'

'You did not.'

'No, I'll be sworn she didn't,' said Hattersley, 'or he'd never look so black.' (TWH 366)

Hargrave effectively accomplishes his own defeat since his black looks authorise Helen's interpretation of events.

To fix still further her own meaning and interpretation of events Helen has recourse to her pen and diary. She offers the diary to Markham to confute the evidence of his senses. Similarly, after discovering her husband's infidelity, she sets about recounting 'the events of the past evening'. She explains that 'I have found relief in describing the very circumstances that have destroyed my peace, as well as the little trivial details attendant upon their discovery' (TWH 317). It is a telling comment. Helen describes the 'very circumstances', really a process of interpreting and fixing those circumstances in an interpretative framework; she amasses 'trivial details' to lend conviction to the interpretation.

This is not to suggest that Anne Brontë is presenting Helen as unreliable. In fact, we implicitly credit her version of events. Rather, Brontë recognises that the Fallen Woman is an interpretation of conventional Victorian society and that what she substitutes in Gilbert's narrative can only be another interpretation, albeit a more 'truthful' one in that it bears greater fidelity to a set of recorded facts. But I would argue that, for all her interest in 'truth', Anne, of the Brontës, was perhaps most aware of its inaccessibility because of her intense religious questioning. The mind of the Creator could not be known and Biblical exegesis was the only avenue to the knowledge possible. Again, because she is committed to a truly moral life and not merely a socially proper or correct life, Anne Brontë presents a radical critique of Victorian society.

Helen, like her author, is also a Biblical exegete, and the ultimate end of all her reading and interpreting is an understanding of the word 'eternal': whether to be damned to eternal hellfire means 'for ever' or 'only till he has paid the uttermost farthing' (TWH 192). Indeed, Helen's story is set by Brontë within this larger questioning of meanings which sees human life as informed by the promise of a hereafter. One's behaviour on earth is regulated by the expectation of a heavenly reward rather than by society's more narrow conventions. Helen amasses passages from all over the Bible in support of her interpretation that 'eternal' means 'long-enduring' but not 'endless'. When her aunt questions, 'Where did you learn all this?', she responds, 'In the Bible, Aunt. I have searched it through, and found nearly thirty passages, all tending to support the same theory' (TWH 191–92). Her aunt follows this reply with the further query, 'And did you find no passages tending to prove the danger and the falsity of such a belief?' (TWH 192). And Helen answers, 'No: I found, indeed, some passages that, taken by themselves, might seem to contradict that opinion; but they will all bear a different construction to that which is commonly given . . .' (TWH 192). For Helen, as no doubt for Anne Brontë contemplating Branwell's damnation, that eternal means only long-enduring 'is a glorious thought to cherish in one's own heart, and I would not part with it for all the world can give!' (TWH 192).

That Anne Brontë may have personally endorsed Helen's 'reading' of Biblical texts is suggested by Charlotte's portrait of her youngest sister in *Shirley*. The character of Caroline Helstone is supposed to be based on Anne even as Shirley Keeldar is based on Emily. At a key point in the novel, the two women are arguing over the interpretation of 'Genesis' with a particularly dogmatic man. Shirley confesses that she was never 'easy in my mind concerning that chapter: it puzzles me', and he responds, 'It is very plain, Miss: he that runs may read'. Suddenly Caroline enters the dialogue with a trenchant observation, surprising for this character: 'He may read it in his own fashion . . . You allow the right of private judgment, I suppose . . . [and] Women may exercise it as well as men?'.[5] Caroline's comments here are surprising in their boldness; usually Caroline will not venture such opinions. But perhaps Charlotte is reproducing Anne's own words at this point, and fidelity to the source accounts for inconsistency in the character.

When Jan Gordon accuses Anne Brontë of *mis*interpreting the Bible in these passages, she seems to miss the point that Anne grasped so fully: no interpretation is definitive.[6] Passages, like episodes, like people, can be read, and the goal is to read with as full a contextual knowledge as possible. Brontë's novel continually works to make that point. Even rumour and speculation are not finally scouted *if* one has weighed the evidence as impartially as possible over a period of time. At the end of the novel, Gilbert Markham, who has vehemently protested the slander directed at Helen Graham, is himself an agent of such slander directed at another. Although he admits he 'cannot prove it', he asserts to Frederick Lawrence that Jane Wilson and Eliza Millward were 'the very originators of the slanderous reports [against Helen Graham] that have

been propagated' (TWH 422). He further claims that Jane
Wilson intends to marry Lawrence, although in the absence
of her statement to that effect, Lawrence reminds Markham
that he has 'no right to make such an assertion respecting
her'. But Markham does not contain his slander even at
this point but adds, 'you think she is singularly charming,
elegant, sensible, and refined: you are not aware that she
is selfish, cold-hearted, ambitious, artful, shallow-minded
– ' (TWH 422). Here, indeed, are contrasting interpretations of a character. And, appropriately, Lawrence
seeks to corroborate one or the other. Gilbert tells us:

> I have reason to believe he pondered my words in
> his mind, eagerly though convertly sought information
> respecting the fair lady from other quarters, secretly
> compared my character of her with what he heard
> from others, and finally came to the conclusion that,
> all things considered, she had much better remain
> Miss Wilson of Ryecote Farm, than be transmuted
> into Mrs Lawrence of Woodford Hall. (TWH 423)

Finally, there must be a preferred or authoritative interpretation simply because one must *act*: Lawrence wants
to take a wife. But always Brontë keeps before us the
importance of defining a reasonable basis for that interpretation and the corollary necessity of cultivating the
ability to read one's situation aright.

## II

This observation leads us to a second major formal and
thematic aspect of *The Tenant of Wildfell Hall:* even as
the novel raises, through structure and subject, the issue of
interpretation and re-presents the Fallen Woman as Exemplary Wife, so, too, it engages the related issue of education

and of that education proper to both sexes. Gilbert Markham must learn to distinguish between an Eliza Millward, the first object of his affections, and Helen Graham just as Helen must distinguish Markham from Huntingdon. Both must learn to recognise what is desirable in a partner. In the process both are educated into the value of possessing reason, discernment, judgement, control, and restraint both for themselves and for their partner. An exploration of this latter point – Brontë's valuation of reason and restraint in both sexes – recalls *Agnes Grey* and Anne Brontë's own ties with the eighteenth century and with Enlightenment feminism, a connection we shall examine more fully in a moment.

Helen Graham, of course, does not instantly captivate Markham. He is confused about what constitutes excellence in a woman, a confusion that stems from the indulgence afforded him as a man. We shall examine the former point first. When Gilbert begins his narrative, he believes his affections are engaged by Eliza Millward, the local vicar's daughter, and he notices Mrs Graham only to criticise. Her lips 'too firmly compressed . . . had something about them that betokened . . . no very soft or amiable temper' (TWH 41). Her eyes have an 'indefinable expression of quiet scorn' (TWH 41). He finds her 'prejudiced against' him (TWH 58). He professes to prefer Eliza's manners – those of a 'pretty, playful kitten' (TWH 42) – full of 'playful nonsense' (TWH 87), although he quickly begins to find her 'rather frivolous, and even a little insipid, compared with the more mature and earnest Mrs Graham' (TWH 73). Markham is caught by Helen's 'depth of thought' (TWH 73). Once caught he is quickly entranced, and he begins what amounts to a courtship carried out by exchanges – of books and of thoughts in conversation – as opposed to the one-way rumour or slander proliferating in the rest of his world. He remarks that 'whenever she did condescend to converse, I liked to listen. Where her opinions and sentiments tallied with mine, it was her extreme good sense, her exquisite taste and feeling that delighted me; where they differed, it was still her uncompromising boldness in the avowal or defence of that difference – her earnestness and keenness that piqued my fancy' (TWH 85). Gilbert's words here reveal his unduly high self-estimate; but they also affirm Helen's intellectual power even as his use of books to gain access to her flatters her intellectual acumen and reveals his more narrow self-interest. He confesses: 'I concluded that the separation could be endured no longer . . . and, taking from the bookcase an old volume that I thought she might be interested in, though, from its unsightly and somewhat dilapidated condition, I had not yet ventured to offer it for her perusal, I hastened away' (TWH 109).

Gilbert's growing appreciation of Helen Graham is the effect first of her personality and second of his own education which is accomplished slowly. Even after Gilbert has apparently learned to recognise reason and judgment as excellent things in a woman, Brontë acquaints us with the limitation of his knowledge through his response to Mary Millward, Eliza's plain sister. Because she is physically unattractive, he finds it impossible to discern her substantial mental virtues. He describes her as a 'plain, sensible girl . . . trusted and valued by her father, loved and courted by all dogs, cats, children, and poor people, and slighted and neglected by everybody else' (TWH 42). Although Helen immediately identifies her as the most worthy resident of Linden-Car, arguing that 'Miss Millward has many estimable qualities, which such as you cannot be expected to perceive or appreciate', Gilbert has already dismissed her: '[she] has the art of conciliating and amusing children . . . if she is good for nothing else' (TWH 88). At the novel's conclusion, Gilbert can measure his own growth by mimicking his society's opinion that it is 'impossible that the plain-looking, plain-dealing, unattractive, unconciliating Miss Millward should ever find a husband' (TWH 441). And we are to recognise that his early, callous responses are a product of the high estimate in which Gilbert holds himself, the effect of a life of being indulged.

Anne Brontë was particularly sensitive to the disastrous effects of such indulgence, a process she had witnessed in her brother, Branwell, whose intemperance was precipitating his early death when Anne was writing *The Tenant of Wildfell Hall*. Brontë reveals in this novel that past indulgence leads not only to moral blindness but even to moral destruction. The same process that has made Gilbert a fop has produced a dissolute reprobate in Huntingdon. *The Tenant of Wildfell Hall* argues even more strenuously against the indulgence of children by parents than does *Agnes Grey*, and it adds a new emphasis. Brontë's second novel reveals the degree to which Victorian society indulges men, and through that indulgence, makes them tyrants over women. In Gilbert, the effects of such indulgence initially may seem fairly innocuous. He is conceited and condescending toward women. His retort to Helen's strenuous and logical defence of equal education for boys and girls is, 'Well! you ladies must always have the last word, I suppose' (TWH 58). The mature Gilbert, who retells these events, can recognise in retrospect: 'I was naturally touchy . . . Perhaps, too, I was a little bit spoiled by my mother and sister, and some other ladies of my acquaintance' (TWH 58). Whereas the young Gilbert can resent 'the degree of maternal admiration' with which his mother regards his brother, he takes as proper that same degree of attention to himself (TWH 37). Late for tea because of his own dalliance, Gilbert nonetheless complains of 'the flavour of the overdrawn tea' and his mother insists that his sister brew a new pot. Rose, in resentment, retorts, '*I'm* nothing at all . . . I'm told I ought not to think of myself – "You know, Rose, in all household matters, we have only two things to consider, first, what's proper to be done, and secondly, what's most agreeable to the gentlemen of the house . . ."' (TWH 79). When Gilbert sensibly complains about the pernicious effects of such indulgence: 'I might sink into the grossest condition of self-indulgence and carelessness about the wants of others, from the mere habit of being constantly cared for myself', his mother blandly asserts, 'it's your business to please yourself, and hers [your wife's] to please you' (TWH 79). Her utmost praise for Gilbert's father is comprised in the comment, 'he was steady and punctual, seldom found fault without a reason, always did justice to my good dinners, and hardly ever spoiled my cookery by delay – and that's as much as any woman can expect of any man' (TWH 79). Ironically, women who suffer most from the indulgence of men are the most culpable in encouraging it.

But faults that might seem minor in Markham assume a menacing dimension in Huntingdon. He initially asks Helen's aunt for permission to marry her niece and begs that she be 'indulgent'. She responds sharply, 'No indulgence for you, . . . must come between me and the consideration of my niece's happiness' (TWH 185). In her idealistic eagerness to marry this man, Helen argues with her aunt that the fault lies with 'a foolish mother who indulged him to the top of his bent, deceiving her husband for him, and doing her utmost to encourage those germs of folly and vice it was her duty to suppress' (TWH 191). Helen enthuses, 'his wife shall undo what his mother did!' (TWH 191). The naïveté of her plan quickly becomes apparent; no restraint can be acceptable to someone who has been indulged for thirty-six years. And not only is his own life at risk but hers and that of her child as well.

Before her son's second birthday, Helen is in 'constant terror . . . lest he should be ruined by that father's thoughtless indulgence'. It is a measure of her self-knowledge that she can admit, 'But I must beware of my own weakness too, for I never knew till now how strong are a parent's temptations to spoil an only child' (TWH 256). Helen, of course, flees from the contamination and steels herself against over-indulgence of her son, both to protect him and to help him cultivate self-restraint. But Huntingdon's down-ward course is unchecked, and Helen returns to a very ill husband out of a sense of duty. At the point she returns, he is not in danger of dying but she notes that 'his long habits of self-indulgence are greatly against him' (TWH 437). Brontë has structured the illness and subsequent death to emphasise the evil effects of indulgence. Even as it is clear that Huntingdon should recuperate, intelligence reaches Gilbert Markham of 'a serious relapse in Mr Huntingdon's illness, entirely the result of his own infatuation in persisting in the indulgence of his appetite for stimulating drink' (TWH 444). Although Huntingdon must pay for his indulgence with his life, the price cannot exact his earlier restraint.

Such indulgence, which Brontë consistently identifies with a male lack of self-restraint, manifests itself on other levels throughout the novel. We recognise it in the dissolute habits and drunken brawls of Huntingdon's friends. We see it in their abuse of their pets and their wives. More problem-atic in terms of Helen's ultimate fate, we find this same lack of restraint in Gilbert Markham. His unprovoked attack on Frederick Lawrence is both irrational and violent. Whatever insult Gilbert imagines he has suffered, his murderous assault seems the act of a madman. And Brontë intends to represent it as such. Gilbert speaks of being prompted by 'some fiend at my elbow' and he experiences 'a feeling of savage satisfaction' (TWH 134). Thematically and structur-ally in the novel, this episode develops the insidious effects of an indulgence that leads to masculine arrogance and abuse of power. It is scarcely consolatory that Markham, from the perspective of twenty years, can recognise 'how I had erred in bringing [Lawrence] into such a condition, and how insultingly my after-services had been offered' (TWH 136). At the moment he attacks and when he after-wards contemplates his action, he is filled with rectitude.

Modern readers have been dissatisfied with Helen's marriage to Markham precisely because he seems different only in degree not in kind from Huntingdon. It is a mark of Brontë's realism, perhaps, that she does not present an ideal hero; she has pointed to the insidious effects of society's indulgence of men, and she will not wholly erase them in any character. However, we should note that the Gilbert who marries Helen Graham is chastened before he can become corrupt.

I have pointed to the effect Helen's diary has in shaping both Gilbert's and our understanding of her and her actions. It serves a second vital function in *educating* Gilbert, an emphasis that links Brontë's *Tenant* with the eighteenth-century novel and with the novels of Jane Austen. Gilbert must submit to the diary's lessons before he can win Helen. After he reads her diary, Helen asks for and receives Gilbert's absolute fidelity to her several injunctions. The Gilbert who marries Helen must accede to her assessment of men and the probity of her 'harshness' in correcting their weakness. Where Helen confesses that her strictness with her husband 'may strike you as harsh', and where that husband charges her with tormenting him through this act of Christian charity 'whereby you hope to gain a higher seat in heaven for yourself, and scoop a deeper pit in hell for me' (TWH 430), Gilbert Markham only praises, 'I see that she was actuated by the best and noblest motives in what she has done' (TWH 435). While Huntingdon rails that he 'should be now abandoned to the mercy of a harsh, exacting, cold-hearted woman like that' (TWH 439), Gilbert enthusiastically anticipates that 'the Millwards and the Wilsons should see, with their own eyes, the bright sun [of Helen] bursting from the cloud – and they should be scorched and dazzled by its beams' (TWH 440).

Anne Brontë has received no praise for the handling of narrative technique here, but it is masterful. Undoubtedly she learned from Emily's *Wuthering Heights* just how effective a framed narrative could be. In Emily's novel Lockwood tells the story of Catherine and Heathcliff and

encloses within his own narrative that part of the tale told by
Nelly Dean. In Anne's *The Tenant of Wildfell Hall*, Gilbert's
perspectives enclose Helen's, but Anne uses this enclosure,
as Emily does not, to enact a major transformation in the
narrator. Gilbert's perspectives merge with Helen's as he
incorporates her letters into his narrative – sometimes
the literal words, sometimes a paraphrase – until the
reader cannot distinguish between them. In Chapter 49,
Gilbert Markham writes, 'The next [letter] was still more
distressing in the tenor of its contents. The sufferer was fast
approaching dissolution . . .' (TWH 449). Theoretically, he
is summarising. But suddenly, we are in the midst of a
scene between Helen and Huntingdon in which present
tense mixes with past to convey immediacy: '"If I try",
said his afflicted wife, "to divert him from these things . . .
it is no better: – 'Worse and worse!' he groans'" (TWH
450). The effect is to make the reader experience an absolute
merging of perspective, and absolute sympathy of minds
that must precede any union between Helen and Gilbert.
And, notably, Helen's interpretation shapes the whole.

   In the economy of the novel, both Gilbert's narrative
of Helen and Helen herself are defined as 'treasures'.
Initially, Gilbert bids adieu to his correspondent, Halford,
using an elaborate monetary metaphor:

> This is the first instalment of my debt. If the coin
> suits you, tell me so, and I'll send you the rest at
> my leisure: if you would rather remain my creditor
> than stuff your purse with such ungainly heavy pieces
> – tell me still, and I'll pardon your bad taste, and
> willingly keep the treasure to myself. (TWH 44)

Huntingdon refers to Helen as a 'treasure': 'I am a
presumptuous dog to dream of possessing such a treasure'
or he says, Helen's father 'would not be willing to part

with such a treasure' (TWH 189). On the one hand, there
is the disturbing implication that a woman is an object of
exchange, having more or less value. This implication is
fully intended as women are 'exchanged' by eager mothers
for monetary gain throughout the novel. On the other
hand, we may recognise in the treasure metaphor the
implication that Helen and the narrative have a value
that can appreciate as the worth of each becomes apparent.
This latter implication is supported in Anne Brontë's
own 'Preface to the Second Edition'. There she claims:

> I wished to tell the truth, for truth always conveys its
> own moral to those who are able to receive it. But as the
> priceless treasure too frequently hides at the bottom of a
> well, it needs some courage to dive for it, especially as he
> that does so will be likely to incur more scorn and oblo-
> quy for the mud and water into which he has ventured to
> plunge, than thanks for the jewel he procures. (TWH 29)

In stirring up the mud of Victorian society, Brontë produces
the treasure of her novel, echoed in the treasure Gilbert's
narrative imparts to Halford, further echoed in the treasure
Helen becomes to Gilbert.

Not only must Gilbert communicate that interpretation to
the world at large but, in marrying Helen, he fully endorses
it. Further, if we examine the proposal scene itself, we see a
man entirely without arrogance, entirely supplicant. Brontë
has structured the narrative so that the death of Helen's
husband immediately precedes the death of her uncle. She
becomes manager of Huntingdon's estate until her son's
maturity and inherits outright her uncle's substantial property, Staningly. Helen has already proved that she can earn
her own living by painting, and she has communicated this
independence of spirit to Esther Hargrave, who announces
her determination to 'run away, and disgrace the family by
earning [her] own livelihood if forced to marry against her

inclination' (TWH 440). Gilbert feels so eclipsed by Helen's ascendency in the world that he stands in the snow outside the gates of Staningly in a 'gloomy reverie' preparing to walk away for ever. Fortuitously, he is discovered and brought inside where Helen proposes by plucking a Christmas rose from a little shrub outside. She compares it to herself: 'This rose is not so fragrant as a summer flower, but it has stood through hardships none of *them* could bear . . . Will you have it?' (TWH 484). Gilbert is so uncertain of where he stands that he cannot take the obvious meaning and thus remains silent until she explains: 'The rose I gave you was an emblem of my heart . . . would you take it away and leave me here alone?' Still unsure, Gilbert asks, 'Would you give me your hand too, if I asked it?' And she responds, with the readers's full sympathy, 'Have I not said enough?' (TWH 485). He is, at this point, a very backward suitor, but he has become what the novel applauds: a man without arrogance and a man full of restraint.

## III

The novel critiques the conventional manly ideal even as it criticises male indulgence. As in *Agnes Grey*, Brontë recognises the extent to which manliness is associated with drinking, swearing and carousing, riding, hunting and killing. Helen relates that the gentlemen 'with boyish eagerness, set out on their expedition against the hapless partridges' (TWH 174). And she observes that, to demonstrate his mettle, one character brags he will 'murder your birds by wholesale' (TWH 199). More serious, however, is the critique of drinking. After witnessing her husband's dissolution, Helen sets out to eradicate any such tendencies in her son. She has poisoned his wine so that it has made him sick and, when they arrive in Linden-Car, he refuses to drink any. For this, she is rebuked by the neighbouring

ladies, 'The poor child will be the veriest milksop that ever
was sopped! Only think what a man you will make of him
...' (TWH 54). She is further criticised because 'you will
treat him like a girl – you'll spoil his spirit, and make a mere
Miss Nancy of him' (TWH 55). When the ladies discern that
Helen plans to teach her son by herself, she is urged against
the 'fatal error . . . of taking that boy's education upon yourself' (TWH 55) And she responds with spirit, 'I am to send
him to school, I suppose, to learn to despise his mother's
authority and affection!' (TWH 55). It is a telling response;
what is at the base of the emphasis on drinking, swearing,
hunting, and killing is fear and contempt for the feminine.

Anne Brontë understands perfectly that, when a man
bonds with his son, he often does so over the body of
the mother. She, the adored object, must be made foolish
and contemptible. Huntingdon's indoctrination of his little
son into boyhood means that he 'learnt to tipple wine like
papa, to swear like Mr Hattersley, and to have his own way
like a man, and [send] mamma to the devil when she tried
to prevent him' (TWH 356). Helen's radical reeducation of
her son parallels the reeducation of Gilbert Markham, and
both underscore Anne Brontë's trenchant critique of male
education and of the whole Victorian patriarchal system.

The critique of male education is accompanied by an
equally radical critique of women's education. I have
already noted the emphasis on reason and rationality in
the presentation of Helen Graham. I linked that emphasis
to an Enlightenment feminism which Anne Brontë came
to through her own religious convictions. The basis of
eighteenth-century arguments for women's equality stressed
woman's possession of a soul capable of redemption.
If women had such a soul, then their reason needed
to be educated, their faculties elevated to make their
redemption possible. Eighteenth-century critics who advo-
cated equality for men and women did not argue – as
feminists do today – for equal access to employment.

Most agreed that women belonged in the home. They did, however, argue for equal access to education in order that a woman fulfill the ends for which she was created.

It is highly unlikely that Anne Brontë would have read Mary Wollstonecraft's *A Vindication of the Rights of Woman* because of the scandal generated by Godwin's publication of his *Memoirs* of Wollstonecraft after she died. Yet the similarity between what Wollstonecraft argues and what Brontë's novel argues is striking. I attribute the similarity to Brontë's own deep sense of divine ends to which individual lives are to be put. In *A Vindication*, Wollstonecraft argues, 'I come round to my old argument; if woman be allowed to have an immortal soul, she must have, as the employment of life, an understanding to improve'.[7] She concludes with the stirring words:

> Gracious Creator of the whole human race! hast thou created such a being as woman, who can trace thy wisdom in thy works, and feel that thou alone art by thy nature exalted above her – for no better purpose? – Can she believe that she was only made to submit to man, her equal, a being, who, like her, was sent into the world to acquire virtue? – Can she consent to be occupied merely to please him; merely to adorn the earth, when her soul is capable of rising to thee? – And can she rest supinely dependent on man for reason, when she ought to mount with him the arduous steeps of knowledge? –[8]

As if in dramatic exemplification of this passage, Huntingdon complains to Helen that she is too absorbed in her devotions so that she does not spare him a glance when he wants her attentions. And Helen retorts, 'What are *you*, sir, that you should set yourself up as a god, and presume to dispute possession of my heart with Him to whom I owe all I have and all I am . . .' (TWH 217). Or, in an argument with Gilbert Markham over the proper education for boys and

girls, Helen questions whether he would apply his rationale
for a boy's education – that he should 'prove all things
by [his] own experience' – to a girl's. When he answers,
'Certainly not', she replies, 'But will you be so good as
to inform me why you make this distinction? Is it that
you think she *has* no virtue?' Helen, like Wollstonecraft,
asserts women's capacity for 'virtue' and in debating
Gilbert raises points reminiscent of those in *A Vindication:*

> It *must* be, either, that you think she is essentially so
> vicious, or so feeble-minded, that she *cannot* withstand
> temptation, – and though she may be pure and innocent
> as long as she is kept in ignorance and restraint, yet,
> being destitute of *real* virtue, to teach her how to sin
> is at once to make her a sinner, and the greater
> her knowledge, the wider her liberty, the deeper will
> be her depravity . . . (TWH 57).

For Helen and Brontë as for Wollstonecraft, virtue must
be educated and the capacity of women for moral education
equals that of men.

To believe women incapable of that education and
to subscribe to the myth that women need protection
from the harsh realities of a competitive business world
is to leave them, ironically, vulnerable to an inescapable
domestic hell of violence, coarseness, and brutality such
as a man like Huntingdon can create. It is only Helen's
education and reason that preserve her 'self-respect and
self-reliance . . . the power, or the will, to watch and guard
herself' (TWH 57). And her developed talent as an artist
ultimately gives her the means of escape and self-support.
The outside world in which Helen succeeds as an artist
is far less threatening than her 'home' at Grass-dale.

Of course, the corollary to the social ideology that
women require protection from a harsh world is the
myth that, because women are 'innocent' of that world,

they can serve as redemptive angels to fallen men. As I pointed out above, Helen is initially seduced by this ideology and expects to 'save' Huntingdon. When her aunt reasonably asks, 'do you imagine your merry, thoughtless profligate would allow himself to be guided by a young girl like you?', Helen responds, 'I think I might have influence sufficient to save him from some errors, and I should think my life well spent in the effort to preserve so noble a nature from destruction' (TWH 165–66). She repeats, 'I will save him', and 'If he has done amiss, I shall consider my life well spent in saving him from the consequences of his early errors' (TWH 167). This idea is so entrancing to Helen that it is perhaps more instrumental than Huntingdon himself in winning her consent to marriage. 'Oh!' she sighs, 'if I could but believe that Heaven has designed me for this!' (TWH 168). Huntingdon, of course, encourages her romance by telling her that 'a little daily talk with [her] would make him quite a saint' (TWH 166) and by claiming that, 'the very idea of having you to care for under my roof would force me to moderate my expenses and live like a Christian – not to speak of all the prudence and virtue you would instil into my mind by your wise counsels and sweet, attractive goodness' (TWH 188). Helen becomes his 'angel' and, more ominously, his 'angel monitress' (TWH 212).

Our discussion of the novel has already made it clear that Anne Brontë explodes this myth as well as the one that women's innocence must be protected by domestic confinement. These are forceful thematic ends of *The Tenant of Wildfell Hall* and help account for the critical attacks it met with when published.

## IV

*The Tenant of Wildfell Hall* would not be the fine novel it is, however, if it engaged us only at the level of theme, as

my analysis to this point may have suggested. *The Tenant*,
like *Agnes Grey*, achieves not only a convincing social
realism but also a compelling psychological realism. Helen
Huntingdon is not simply 'good', in the mode of some of
Charles Dickens's pure heroines; she is a woman of passion
and vacillation – a fully credible, struggling individual.

Helen not only fails to redeem Huntingdon from his
downward course, but, ironically, he begins to ensnare
her in his fall. Here, Brontë picks up a theme introduced in her poem 'Self-Communion' and in *Agnes Grey*
– society's contamination of the pure spirit – but now it
receives more powerful and compelling development:

I see that time, and toil, and truth
An inward hardness can impart, –
Can freeze the generous blood of youth,
And steel full fast the tender heart. (P 155)

This becomes Helen's cruel lesson in *The Tenant*, as Anne
Brontë demonstrates a compelling depth of psychological
insight that makes the novel truly powerful and underscores
the greatness therein.

We have noted that Helen launches her marriage full
of hopes for the redemption she will enact in Huntingdon.
But he remains impervious to her influence while subtly
and sickeningly she falls prey to the coarse personalities surrounding her, gradually discovering a growing
corruption in her own nature. She laments:

. . . since he and I are one, I so identify myself
with him, that I feel his degradation, his failings,
and transgressions as my own . . . I am familiarised
with vice and almost a partaker in his sins. Things
that formerly shocked and disgusted me, now seem only
natural. I know them to be wrong, because reason and

God's word declare them to be so; but I am gradually
losing that instinctive horror and repulsion which was
given me by nature, or instilled into me by the precepts
and example of my aunt. (TWH 273–74)

She rails, 'how shall I get through the months or years
of my future life, in company with that man – my greatest
enemy – for none could injure me as he has done' (TWH
318). Or she cries out, 'I hate him tenfold more than
ever, for having brought me to this – God pardon me
for it – and all my sinful thoughts! Instead of being
humbled and purified by my afflictions, I feel that they
are turning my nature to gall' (TWH 323). In this portrait
of a woman struggling with an ideal self-conception against
a powerful and pervasive social corruption, we discover
genius of portraiture. A less insightful writer would have
allowed Helen to remain static and pure.

Instead we are given a dynamic personality, capable of
Christian idealism, being tested by self–doubt and engaged
in a struggle with self and belief. But Anne Brontë
does not stop here. With brilliant insight, she recognises
that, for all of Helen's virtues, her nature partly fuels
Huntingdon's self-destruction because their personalities
are incompatible. In closely detailed, realistic domestic
scenes, Anne Brontë unfolds the destructive interaction
between Helen and her husband.

Helen becomes a scourge to her husband; in her incessant
lecturing aimed at his moral improvement, she both alien-
ates him and hastens his ruin. She early begins to quell her
impulses to chasten 'lest I should disgust him with . . . me'
(TWH 220). But she often indulges these impulses. After a
major quarrel, Helen deliberately preserves her equanimity
even though her husband is searching for 'traces of tears' so
that he can initiate a reconciliation. She notes, 'I determined
he should make the first advances, or at least show some
signs of an humble and contrite spirit, first; for, if I began,

it would only minister to his self-conceit, increase his arrogance, and quite destroy the lesson I wanted to give him' (TWH 224). Having married Huntingdon clearly believing she is his moral superior, Helen falls prey to a rectitude that galls rather than arouses a desire for emulation. Even in a fond mood, Huntingdon warns Helen she may drive him from her by 'too much severity'; remember, he says, that 'I am a poor, fallible mortal'. He jokingly refers to Helen as his 'saint'. Annabella, Huntingdon's mistress, confronts Helen over their relative effects on the man and points out: 'I know you did your utmost to deliver him from [his vices] – but without success . . . . Take care of him when I am gone and [don't], by harshness and neglect, drive him back to his old courses' (TWH 327).

The psychologically rich relationship between husband and wife is further developed with the birth of a son. He becomes a focus of their contest. Although Freud has made much of the son's jealousy of the father, Anne Brontë gives a convincing protrait of the father's jealousy and resentment of the son. Huntingdon complains, 'I shall positively hate that little wretch, if you worship it so madly!' (TWH 253) and 'At present it is nothing more than a little selfish, senseless sensualist' (TWH 255). Ironically, he describes himself, and his comments provide insight into his own nature and thereby explain his resentment and sense of displacement. Helen, the angel monitress, stands in the role of 'mother' to Huntingdon.

Ultimately, Huntingdon realises that the best way to attack, undermine, and defeat Helen is to corrupt his son. Helen laments:

> Thus, not only have I the father's spirit in the son to contend against, the germs of his evil tendencies to search out and eradicate, and his corrupting intercourse and example in after-life to counteract, but already *he* counteracts my arduous labour for the child's advantage, destroys my

influence over his tender mind, and robs me of his very love; – I had no earthly hope but this, and he seems to take a diabolical delight in tearing it away. (TWH 333)

This kind of pernicious leverage could well kindle motives of revenge in the most Christian of hearts.

We might conclude, then, that Helen's desire to redeem Huntingdon is not entirely selfless, a fact that emerges most forcefully in his deathbed sequences. Hearing that he is very ill, Helen returns to Grass-dale to nurse her husband. In this action, she and Gilbert Markham, as I've pointed out above, acknowledge only generous motives, particularly concern for the state of Huntingdon's soul. We recall that Gilbert enthusiastically praises Helen: 'I see that she was actuated by the best and noblest motives . . .' (TWH 435). We know that redemption was a subject close to Anne Brontë's heart, and that she broke radically with religious convention in suggesting that there was no sin so black that it could not ultimately be purged away. And she dramatises this conviction in *The Tenant of Wildfell Hall,* but her intuitive grasp of the psychological complexities underlying quotidian reality prevents her giving us mere dogma. Instead Brontë depicts a vivid drama of clashing personalities where purity of motive is contaminated by the very situation in which it must demonstrate itself. We cannot help but remember that Huntingdon's friends have described her as a 'she-tiger' or 'vixen' in her relationship to her husband (269). Hattersley confesses, 'He's afraid of you, to be sure' (TWH 301). When Helen returns to her husband's bedside, she is as much avenging demon as she is redeeming angel. Huntingdon at first refuses to recognise her, preferring to believe she is a 'fancy' because, 'I can't stand such a mania as this; it would kill me!' He pleads, 'For God's sake, don't torment me now!' and when she insists he recognise that she is real, he replies, 'Oh! I see . . . it's an act of Christian charity, whereby you hope to gain a higher seat in heaven for yourself, and scoop a deeper pit in hell for me' (TWH 430). With death imminent, Huntingdon continues to challenge the purity of Helen's motives, her willingness to 'do anything [she] can to relieve him'. He rails: 'Yes, *now*, my immaculate angel; but when once you have secured your reward, and find yourself safe in heaven, and me howling in hell-fire, catch you lifting a finger to serve me *then*!' (TWH 446).

This masterfully depicted interaction reveals that, in psychological terms, Helen has achieved 'innocent' revenge. She is punishing with impunity. Her motives in returning to her husband cannot be impugned, but her presence is deadly to him. He cries, 'you never hoped for such a glorious opportunity!' and adds, 'Oh, yes, you're wonderous gentle and obliging! – But you've driven me mad with it all!' (TWH 433). Finally, he defines her victory: 'Oh, this [is] sweet revenge! . . . And you can enjoy it with such a quiet conscience too, because it's all in the way of duty' (TWH 433). Ultimately, of course, he becomes docile in her hands, admitting, 'Oh, Helen, if I had listened to you, it never would have come to this!' and 'I'm sorry to have wronged you, Nell, because you're so good to me' (TWH 448–450). She has won complete vindication from her husband. The reader, however, has the benefit of distance from the scene and is impressed by the degree to which corrupt situations corrupt 'pure' intentions. The reader is invited to contemplate the problem of Christian action in a fuller universe.

It would be wrong to suggest that Anne Brontë did not take seriously the redemption of Huntingdon. She does, but her commitment to truth allows her to dramatise the way in which the Christian impulse may become entangled in the medium of social reality and contending psychologies and thereby be compromised and contaminated.

The structural, thematic, and psychological richness of this novel should have earned for it a greater reputation than it has. George Moore early gave the novel high praise, identifying in it the 'quality of heat, one of the rarest qualities, which taken together with all her other qualities, would, had she lived ten years longer, have given her a place beside Jane Austen, perhaps even a higher place.'[9] The compliment is deserved.

The reader of Anne Brontë's novels must ask what makes great art, what it is that determines the estimate in which we hold a work. Is it historical accident or something inherent in the novel? The answer to such questions is neither easy nor obvious. Yet, surely, novels that can be read and reread with pleasure, that can generate interest in their themes, that can elicit attention to their innovative techniques, and that can do so at a highly sophisticated level, surely such works deserve the designation of 'great'.

Anne Brontë's *The Tenant of Wildfell Hall* engages us, through complex and psychologically convincing characters, in an action that uses a series of embedded narratives to underscore its central themes of interpretation, evidence and conclusions, of gossip, reliability and belief, and of reason, education and virtue. Finally, in their synthesis of possibility and actuality, of vision and reality, the embedded narratives encourage and enable the reader's own discernment, interpretation, and reeducation. It is a signal achievement.

# 6 Critics on Anne Brontë: a 'literary Cinderella'

The historical problem for the critic of Anne Brontë – as should by now be clear – is to acknowledge the extent of her indebtedness to her sisters and to her milieu while also recognising the scope of her contributions. That is, Anne's art is shaped by its context without being confined by it; it is also distinctive, innovative, and influential, especially so on Charlotte. Anne not only took her subjects and techniques from her world, but, like all creative artists, she transformed them.

The fact that the three Brontë sisters first published their poems jointly and then that Anne's and Emily's first novels made up one volume initially encouraged critics to treat them comparatively and to question whether they were, indeed, three different writers. Both of these tendencies had consequences for later evaluations of the sisters' works.

In comparative analyses, Anne's work has tended to receive both less attention and less praise. The critical assumption has been that her work is not of the calibre of her sisters' – an assumption that has persisted to the present. But Anne has also garnered praise from serious critics, and our preceding analysis should suggest that Anne's work – harkening back to seventeenth- and eighteenth-century models – would have been less congenial to the tastes of the early reviewers who set the critical pattern. Also the boldness of the realistic representation in *The Tenant of Wildfell Hall* proved as offensive to contemporaneous tastes as did the romanticised gothicism of *Wuthering Heights*. The publication of *The Tenant*, in fact, intensified the negative commentary on all of the Brontë novels. But an attention to the literary context of Anne's work and to the historical context of her publication allows us to begin to revise the image of Anne as a pale shadow of her sisters.

The poetry of the three 'Bells' generally received scant though encouraging reviews. The *Critic* praised the work of all the Bells and singled out Anne's 'Vanitas Vanitatum' as reminiscent 'of some quaint but powerful productions of the close of the Elizabethan Age'.[1] Emily's poetry was often distinguished as the most significant and praise-worthy – and there time has borne out that judgment – but Anne and Charlotte both received favourable notice.

When the novels were published, the tendency toward joint and comparative reviewing had more serious conse-quences for Anne. *Agnes Grey*, although antecedent to *Jane Eyre* in composition, was published after Charlotte's novel, and appeared in one volume with *Wuthering Heights*. Inevi-tably *Agnes Grey*, which actually influenced *Jane Eyre*, was seen as a weak imitation. *Douglas Jerrold's Weekly Newspaper* claims that '*Agnes Grey* is a tale well worth the writing and the reading' yet describes the heroine as 'a sort of younger sister to *Jane Eyre*; but inferior to her in every way' (CH 227). Anne suffered, too, in the comparison with Emily. On the one hand, critics have argued that Anne's *Agnes Grey* received more notice than it might otherwise have done were it not linked to *Wuthering Heights*. Yet we must also note that the raw power of Emily's novel led critics to concentrate on it, often to the exclusion of Anne's. Several reviews ignored *Agnes Grey*; others mentioned it only in passing. A reviewer in the *Spectator* recognises that Anne's novel is not so 'ex-treme' as Emily's, then adds, 'but what it gains in measure

is possibly lost in power' (CH 217). The *Athenaeum* notes,
too, that '*Agnes Grey* is more acceptable to us, though less
powerful' (CH 219). Finally, one unsigned notice in the *Atlas*
spends several pages on *Wuthering Heights* before turning to
*Agnes Grey*, 'a story of very different stamp . . . Perhaps
we shall best describe it as a somewhat coarse imitation of
one of Miss Austin's [sic] charming stories'. The reviewer
concludes, 'the story, though lacking the power and originality of *Wuthering Heights*, is infinitely more agreeable. It
leaves no painful impression on the mind – some may think
it leaves no impression at all' (CH 233). It is a curious
conclusion that damns with faint praise. We must recognise,
however, that the virtues of *Agnes Grey*, with its emphasis
on realism and its quiet understatement, would be utterly
eclipsed when put in the context of *Wuthering Heights*. In
addition, the taste of the age for tales of high romance
would also predispose readers against Anne's subtle story.

The reception of all the Brontë novels changed key
with the publication of *The Tenant of Wildfell Hall*, in
part as a consequence of Newby's deliberate attempt to
confuse the identities of the Bells and to claim for Anne
authorship of *Jane Eyre*. E. P. Whipple's review of the Bell
novels for *North American Review* attacked the 'whole firm
of Bell & Co. [who] seem to have a sense of the depravity
of human nature peculiarly their own'. He continues,
'This is especially the case with Acton Bell [sic], the
author of *Wuthering Heights*, *The Tenant of Wildfell Hall*,
and, if we mistake not, of certain offensive but powerful
portions of *Jane Eyre*' (CH 247). But if the Brontës found
themselves under attack for crudity and coarseness, they
also received recognition for powerful effects. Anne's new
novel joined Emily's and Charlotte's in gathering praise.
The reviewer in the *Spectator* noted that '*The Tenant of
Wildfell Hall*, like its predecessor, suggests the idea of
considerable abilities ill applied. There is power, effect,
and even nature, though of an extreme kind, in its pages'

(CH 250). The *Athenaeum* cited Anne's novel as 'the most interesting novel which we have read for a month past' (CH 251). Finally, Anne's works compelled admiration for their genius of representation. The American reviewer of *Literary World* concludes by elevating Anne Brontë above Dickens:

> However objectionable these works may be to crude minds which cannot winnow the chaff of vulgarity from the rich grain of genius which burdens them, very many, while enjoying the freshness and vigor, will gladly hail their appearance, as boldly and eloquently developing blind places of wayward passion in the human heart, which is far more interesting to trace than all the bustling lanes and murky alleys through which the will-o'-the-wisp genius of Dickens has so long led the public mind. (CH 261)

These reviews, coupled with the brisk sales of *The Tenant*, should have established the novel among those that endured. George Moore later blamed Charlotte for Anne's loss of reputation and, although it is unfair to Charlotte to try to pin the blame on her, it is equally unfair to Anne to let a verdict of artistic inferiority stand unchallenged. Certainly, Charlotte's own comments on the novel after Anne's death are at best faint praise, and she allowed her dislike of the novel to keep it out of print for a decade following Anne's death.

Miriam Allott has noted that perhaps it was Charlotte's preoccupation with Whipple's negative review that led her to accuse critics of treating her sisters' (and, by implication, her own) works harshly, an accusation she makes in her 'Biographical Notice' for the 1850 edition of *Wuthering Heights* and *Agnes Grey*.[2] More significant, it was probably this review that also led Charlotte to denigrate Anne's achievement in *The Tenant of Wildfell Hall*.

Charlotte would have had several reasons for minimising Anne's achievement in *The Tenant*. First, in the character of Huntingdon, the novel may have painfully recalled Branwell's degradation. Second, Charlotte blamed the novel for Anne's own decline, asserting that 'hers was naturally a sensitive, reserved, and dejected nature; what she saw sank very deeply into her mind; it did her harm'.[3] Third, if Charlotte felt that *The Tenant of Wildfell Hall* was a critique of *Jane Eyre*, as I argue in Chapter 2, then she may have wished to suppress that critique. Finally, and perhaps most significant, Charlotte may have unconsciously blamed Anne's novel for a number of attacks on *Jane Eyre*'s coarseness. The reviewer in the *Rambler*, for example, had concluded that, 'Nevertheless, on the whole, we should say that *The Tenant of Wildfell Hall* is not so *bad* a book as *Jane Eyre*' (CH 268).

It was Charlotte who initiated a second stage of criticism to her sisters' novels and who consolidated an approach to the three authors. Basically, she dismissed *The Tenant of Wildfell Hall*, claiming that 'the choice of subject was an entire mistake. Nothing less congruous with the writer's nature could be conceived.'[4] Since this notice preceded the re-publication of *Agnes Grey*, it was implicitly asserting that Anne's first novel demonstrated the proper province and, ultimately limitation, of her talents, a limitation underscored by Charlotte's comparison of her two sisters: 'Anne's character was milder and more subdued; she wanted the power, the fire, the originality of her sister [Emily], but was well endowed with quiet virtues of her own.'[5] None of this commentary helped Anne's reputation.

It is worth pausing briefly to reflect on what might have been Anne's fate had *The Tenant of Wildfell Hall* been re-published with *Agnes Grey* so that critics could re-acquaint themselves with Anne's greater novel and so that critics could take that opportunity to measure the substantial artistic growth between the two novels. Charlotte herself never accomplished Anne's imaginative range. Further, Anne was only twenty-eight when she wrote *The Tenant of Wildfell Hall;* at a comparable age, Charlotte had produced only *The Professor.* And yet, despite the disadvantages in representation Anne suffered at Charlotte's hands, G. H. Lewes could still link the youngest sister with Emily in his 1850 review in the *Leader*:

> Currer Bell's riper mind enables her to paint with a freer hand; nor can we doubt but that her two sisters, had they lived, would also have risen into greater strength and clearness, retaining the extraordinary power of vigorous delineation which makes their writings so remarkable. (CH 292)

In 1930, George Moore would claim that, had Anne lived, she could have taken a place beside Jane Austen or even higher.[6] Perhaps the claim seems exaggerated, but it should help us to see that, whatever place we ultimately accord to Anne, she has, to date, remained underestimated.

Mrs Gaskell's biography of Charlotte Brontë, published in 1857, basically reiterated Charlotte's estimates of her sisters and, in generating antagonism with the Robinson family, foreclosed any opportunities to learn valuable information about Anne during those crucial five years at Thorp Green as the Robinsons' governess. In the reviews that followed the publication of Gaskell's *Life of Charlotte Brontë* we discover three tendencies: first, to echo Charlotte's and Mrs Gaskell's estimates of Emily and Anne; second, a more generous but more infrequent course, to project a body of substantial achievements that might have come from Anne and Emily had they not died so young; and third, to account biographically for Anne's novels and so discredit their artistry.

Charlotte's and Mrs Gaskell's characterisation of Anne as mild and gentle, as less 'original' than Emily resonates in Peter Bayne's 1857 review – 'she possessed no such strong genius as her sister' (CH 326) – and in John Skelton's review of the same year – 'In Acton's [poetry], indeed, there is more of the ordinary woman, mild, patient, devout, loving' (CH 334) – and in an unsigned review in the *Christian Remembrancer* – 'Anne was not unnatural' (CH 369). In these interpretations we see the beginnings of the Brontë myth in which Anne plays the quiet sister whose role is that of foil to the genius of her more gifted siblings.

Not all critics subscribed to this myth. Emile Montegut recognised the greatness of which Anne as well as Emily might yet have been capable: 'I would like to say a word about the talent of Miss Brontë's sisters . . . These two remarkable people, whose works have not been esteemed at their true value, having been as it were buried under Charlotte's success, deserve more space than we can give them' (CH 376). And Margaret Sweat writing for the *North American Review*, had the penetration to see that Anne 'was gentle chiefly through contrast with her Spartan sisters, and that the savage elements about her found an occasional echo from within' (CH 384).

During the remainder of the nineteenth century, critics settled into a consensus about Anne, following Charlotte's lead in the 'Biographical Notice' and Mrs Gaskell's details in the *Life*: Anne's novels were basically autobiographical, written out of a grim sense of duty and therefore devoid of artistry. T. W. Reid commented in 1877 that, 'Branwell's fall formed the dark turning-point in Anne Brontë's life. So it was not unnatural that it should colour her literary labours' (CH 403). Swinburne, too, writing on Emily Brontë gestured briefly toward Anne: 'The impression of this miserable experience [Branwell's degradation] is visible only in Anne Brontë's second work . . . which deserves perhaps a little more notice and recognition than it has ever received' (CH 440). Swinburne's praise seems almost an afterthought.

Finally, Mary Ward, who wrote prefaces to the Haworth edition of the Brontë novels in 1898, firmly entrenches this interpretation of *The Tenant* in the critical mind. Although

Ward's criticism has been praised for its 'breadth and sense of proportion', it is hard to read her comments on Anne as anything more than a rehashing of Charlotte and Mrs Gaskell.[7] Ward begins her commentary on the youngest sister by noting that the 'books and poems that she wrote serve as matter of comparison by which to test the greatness of her two sisters. She is the measure of their genius – like them, yet not with them' (CH 458). Her assessment of the novels follows:

> But Anne was not strong enough, her gift was not vigorous enough, to enable her thus to transmute experience and grief . . . It did not much affect the writing of *Agnes Grey*, which was completed in 1846, and reflected the minor pains and discomforts of her teaching experience, but it combined with the spectacle of Branwells' increasing moral and physical decay to produce that bitter mandate of conscience under which she wrote *The Tenant of Wildfell Hall*. (CH 459)

Ward's conclusion – 'It is not as the writer of *Wildfell Hall*, but as the sister of Charlotte and Emily Brontë, that Anne Brontë escapes oblivion' (CH 460) – seems to have dominated critical thought into the twentieth century.

For example, although W. T. Hale deserves credit for writing a monograph on Anne Brontë in 1929 and implicitly claiming her importance by granting her individual study, explicitly he echoes Mrs Ward: 'Anne, indeed, will never be known to fame either as novelist or poet, but only as the sister of Charlotte and Emily.'[8] Hale's chauvinistic commentary underlines the need for the corrective of a feminist approach. Hale emphasises Anne's need – a 'woman's' need – for love and ignores a 'woman's' need for accomplishment and Anne's own intensely expressed desire to be allowed to live to pursue her talents, her determination that 'Such humble talents as God has given me I will endeavour to put to their greatest use' (TWH 30). Hale concludes, 'The Gods were not kind to her: no men except her father's curates ever had a chance to look at her. But the gods must have loved her, after all, for they did not prolong her agony. They let her die young'.[9] It is hard to find this conclusion other than offensive; following this logic we might argue that *all* the Brontës would have been fortunate to have died in childhood with Maria and Elizabeth.

The notable exception to this sentimental biographising of Anne's art, of course, is George Moore who in *Conversations in Ebury Street*, published in 1930, asserts Anne's great talents. Moore focused on the artistry of Anne Brontë's novels, characterising *Agnes Grey* as 'a prose narrative simple and beautiful as a muslin dress' and identifying in *The Tenant of Wildfell Hall* the rare literary quality of 'heat'.[10] Moore blamed Charlotte for Anne's depreciation and accused the older sister of plagiarising the younger's works. This accusation seems extreme, but certainly we have identified in Chapter 2 significant indebtedness.

Interest in Anne's work received another boost in 1959 when Winifred Gérin published her definitive biography (of which a new edition was published in 1976), and Ada Harrison and Derek Stanford published *Anne Brontë: Her life and Work*, the first sustained study of Anne's poetry and novels. The mid- and late sixties saw an increasing interest in considering the sisters within their family and historical context, an interest reflected in W. A. Craik's *The Brontë Novels* (1968) and Inga-Stina Ewbank's *Their Proper Sphere: A Study of the Brontë Sisters as Early Victorian Female Novelists* (1966). But Miriam Allott astutely notes that 'Anne's present-day status is perhaps still best indicated by the implication in Norman Sherry's title for his introductory primer, *The Brontës: Charlotte and Emily* (1969)'[11]

The two critics who have done most to call attention to Anne Brontë's artistry in the past decade are Edward Chitham who meticulously edited Anne's poetry in 1979, and P. J. M. Scott who published in 1983 *Anne Brontë: A New Critical Assessment*. Scott's book is stronger on the poetry than on the novels, and there remains a tendency to fault Brontë's technique rather than to expand his own critical frame of reference. In addition, it tends to be descriptive rather than analytical so it fails to do justice to Anne Brontë's innovative themes and techniques and it is not sensitive to the rich feminist dimension of the texts.

In addition to editing the poetry, Edward Chitham has also written an analysis of the ways in which *The Tenant of Wildfell Hall* revises *Wuthering Heights* and has thereby encouraged our perception of Anne as an innovative artist. His essay is part of a collaborative effort with Tom Winnifrith, *Brontë Facts and Brontë Problems* (1983), which, by seeking to correct some biographical and critical misdirections in Brontë scholarship, allows Anne to emerge more fully as an independent personality.

The feminist critics, who have been so generally successful in revising our literary appreciation and critical estimate of women writers, especially those in the Victorian period, have had surprisingly little to say about Anne Brontë. While Charlotte has benefited immensely by the feminist perspective, Anne is little better known and scarcely more frequently discussed than she was previously. Patricia Spacks, *The Female Imagination*, does not mention her and Elaine Showalter, *A Literature of Their Own*, makes only one passing reference to Anne. Ellen Moers, *Literary Women*, and Sandra Gilbert and Susan Gubar, *The Madwoman in the Attic*, are both briefly interested in the image of the woman as painter in *The Tenant of Wildfell Hall*, but taking the image out of context, these critics do not do justice to the radical nature of Anne's presentation. Indeed, Charlotte's novels provided the impetus for Gilbert's and Gubar's study and to read Anne in the light of Charlotte is partially to misread her. Nina Auerbach's *Woman and the Demon* does not address

Brontë's novels, although *The Tenant of Wildfell Hall* presents a compelling instance of woman's transformative powers that Auerbach might have addressed. In *Communities of Women* Auerbach does look at Anne in the context of the family as does Elizabeth Hardwick in *Seduction and Betrayal*, but, again, neither critic discusses Anne's novels. Most recently, Margaret Homans in *Bearing the Word:Language and Female Experience in Nineteenth-Century Women's Writing* makes no reference to Anne although Anne was one of the first women writers to adopt a woman as narrator.

I suggested earlier that Anne Brontë may stand, *vis-à-vis* her sisters, as the woman writer usually stands in patriarchy. That is, the woman writer's perspectives and values and achievements are not properly evaluated, only seen as deficient in light of other, usually male standards. In the case of the Brontës, Emily's and Charlotte's novels have set the standard for judgment while Anne's work, which departs from theirs, has failed to find a consistently appreciative audience. But Anne Brontë's is an important voice in the novel, and it has been the purpose of this book to define that importance for the development of the novel, for theory of the novel, and for feminist criticism. The final goal of this study must be to encourage readers to evaluate Anne Brontë for themselves and then, one hopes, revise Mary Ward's assessment of Anne – 'like them [Emily and Charlotte], yet not with them' – to 'unlike them, yet with them'.

# Note on Texts

(AG) *Agnes Grey*, Everyman's Library (London and Melbourne, Dent, 1958).
(P) *The Poems of Anne Brontë A New Text and Commentary* (ed.) Edward Chitham (London and Basingstoke, Macmillan, 1979).
(TWH) *The Tenant of Wildfell Hall* (Harmondsworth, Penguin, 1979).
(LL) *The Brontës Their Lives, Friendships and Correspondence* (eds) T. J. Wise and J. A. Symington, 4 vols (Oxford, Shakespeare Head, 1934).

# Notes

## Notes to Chapter 1

1. See Phillip Rhodes, 'A Medical Appraisal of the Brontës', *Brontë Society Transactions*, 16, 2 (1971).

2. Winifred Gérin, *Anne Brontë* (London, Allen Lane, 1959; 1976), Ch. 4, especially pp. 33–34.

3. *The Poems of Anne Brontë: A New Text and Commentary* (ed.) Edward Chitham (London and Basingstoke, Macmillan, 1979), p. 153. All further references appear in the text abbreviated as P.

4. Quoted in Winifred Gérin, op. cit., p. 13.

5. *The Brontës: Their Lives, Friendships and Correspondence* (eds.) T. J. Wise and J. A. Symington (Oxford, Shakespeare Head, 1934), 1I, p. 338. All further references appear in the text abbreviated as LL.

6. Elizabeth Gaskell, *The Life of Charlotte Brontë* (Harmondsworth, Penguin, 1975), p. 94.

7. Winifred Gérin, op. cit., pp. 18, 86.

8. Winifred Gérin, *Branwell Brontë* (Toronto and New York, Thomas Nelson and Sons, 1961), p. 17.

9 .*The Tenant of Wildfell Hall* (Harmondsworth, Penguin, 1979), p. 27. All further references appear in the text abbreviated as TWH.

10. Quoted in Winifred Gérin, *Branwell Brontë*, op. cit., p. 82.

11. Quoted in Elizabeth Gaskell, op. cit., p. 117.

12. Cited in Winifred Gérin, *Anne Brontë*, op. cit., p. 86.

13. See Edward Chitham and Tom Winnifrith, *Brontë Facts and Brontë Problems* (London, Macmillan, 1983), pp. 20–33 for a comprehensive discussion of problems in early Brontë chronology.

14. Quoted in Winifred Gérin, *Anne Brontë*, op. cit., p. 101.

15. Juliet Barker makes this argument in her edition of *The Brontës' Selected Poems* (London, J. M. Dent, 1985), p. 145.

16. Anne Brontë's Prayer Book, Brontë Parsonage Museum.

17. Winifred Gérin, *Anne Brontë*, op. cit., p. 286.

18. *Agnes Grey* (London, J. M. Dent, 1982), p. 53. All further references appear in the text abbreviated as AG.

19. Rita McWilliams-Tullberg, 'Women and Degrees at Cambridge University', in *A Widening Sphere: Changing Roles of Victorian Women* (ed.) Martha Vicinus (Bloomington, Indiana University Press, 1977), pp. 117–45.

20. Virginia Woolf, 'Professions for Women', in *The Death of the Moth and Other Essays* (New York, Harcourt Brace Jovanovich 1942), pp. 235–42.

## Notes to Chapter 2

1. George Moore, *Conversations in Ebury Street* (New York, Boni and Liveright, 1924), p. 260.

2. Pauline Nestor, *Charlotte Brontë* (London, Macmillan, 1987), p. 28.

3. Samuel Johnson, *Rasselas* (Harmondsworth, Penguin, 1976), p. 95.

4. I am grateful to Margaret Kirkham, *Jane Austen, Feminism and Fiction* (Brighton, Harvester Press, 1983), p. xii for pointing out the connection between an emphasis on reason and Enlightenment feminism.

5. Ibid., p. 10.

6. Hannah More, *Moral Sketches of Prevailing Opinions and Manners*, 3rd ed. (London, T. Cadell and W. Davies, 1819), p. 76. This edition, which I consulted in the Brontë Parsonage Museum, belonged to Anne Brontë and someone, although it may not be Anne, has marked the passage I quote.

7. Edward Chitham, 'Diverging Twins: Some Clues to *Wildfell Hall*', in Chitham and Winnifrith, op. cit., pp. 94–5.

8. Charlotte Brontë, *Jane Eyre* (New York, W.W. Norton, 1971), pp. 304, 321, 330, 332, 350, 361, 362, 363, 366.

9. Ibid., p. 398.

10. Ibid., p. 368.

11. Miriam Allot (ed.), *The Brontës: The Critical Heritage* (London and Boston, Routledge and Kegan Paul, 1974), p. 274. All further references appear in the text abbreviated as CH.

12. Jan Gordon, 'Gossip, Diary, Letter, Text: Anne Brontë's Narrative Tenant and the Problematic of the Gothic Sequel', *English Literary History* 5, 4 (1984), p. 740.

13. 'Biographical Notice', in Emily Brontë, *Wuthering Heights* (ed.) William M. Sale, Jr. (New York, W. W. Norton, 1963), p. 8.

14. Edward Chitham, 'Diverging Twins', op. cit., p. 100.

15. Charlotte Brontë, op. cit., p. 274.

16. Ibid., p. 277.

17. Ibid., p. 277.

18. Pauline Nestor, op. cit., p. 34.

19. Sandra Gilbert and Susan Gubar, *The Madwoman in the Attic: The Woman Writer and the Nineteenth-Century Literary Imagination* (New Haven and London: Yale University Press, 1979), p. 82, argue that 'Even when she becomes a professional artist, Helen continues to fear the social implications of her vocation. Associating female creativity with freedom from male domination, and dreading the misogynistic censure of her community, she produces art that at least partly hides her experience of her actual place in the world'. This reading seems misguided. As we have seen, Helen shows no fear of the 'social implications of her vocation', and she hides her 'experience of her actual place in the world' so her errant husband cannot find her and force her to return home.

20. I again differ from Gilbert and Gubar, ibid., p. 82, who claim that Brontë's Helen Graham 'is prototypical, since we shall see that women artists are repeatedly attracted to the Satanic/Byronic hero even while they try to resist the sexual submission exacted by this oppressive younger son who seems, at first, so like a brother or double'. I argue in my Chapter 5 that the source of attraction for Helen is not a sexual masochism but a social idealism. One could argue for both except that Helen is revolted by Huntingdon's attempts at coercion.

21. Pauline Nestor, op. cit., p. 35.

22. George Moore, op. cit., p. 261.

23. Ibid., p. 261.

## Notes to Chapter 3

1. Poet Richard Howard has noted this capacity of dramatic monologues. Cited in *The Norton Anthology of Literature*, (eds) Abrams et al., 4th ed., vol. 2 (New York, W. W. Norton, 1979), p. 1229.

2. Edward Chitham develops a similar argument, *Poems*, op. cit., p. 169.

3. See, for example, Carol Gilligan, *In a Differnt Voice* (Cambridge, Harvard University Press, 1982).

4. I am grateful to my colleague Alistair Duckworth for these observations.

5. Edward Chitham, *Poems*, op. cit., p. 176, has carefully studied dates of composition in his edition of the poems and makes this observation.

6. 'Biographical Notice', op. cit., pp. 6–7.

7. I am grateful to Edward Chitham, *Poems*, op. cit., p. 181, for this observation.

8. Edward Chitham, ibid., p. 194, has looked at rhyme in 'Self-Communion' and he notes: 'An analysis of the first forty-six lines shows the economy noted in earlier poems: of thee lines eight end in

the sound *ears*, four more in the sound *air/ere*, and six in the sound *ay*. Thus eighteen out of forty-six lines end with similar sounds. This strong concentration effects an arresting plangency, and the predominance of long vowels and diphthongs throughout continues this tone'.

## Notes to Chapter 4

1. Charlotte Brontë, op. cit., p. 96.

2. Winifred Gérin, *Anne Brontë*, op. cit., p. 176.

3. Jane Austen, *Pride and Prejudice* (Harmondsworth, Penguin, 1972), p. 370.

4. Charlotte Brontë, *Shirley* (Harmondsworth, Penguin, 1974), p. 224.

5. Ibid., p. 225.

6. Ibid., p. 436.

7. Ibid., p. 531.

## Notes to Chapter 5

1. Caroline Norton, 'A Letter to the Queen on Lord Chancellor Cranworth's Marriage and Divorce Bill', in *Victorian Women: A Documentary Account* (eds) Hallerstein et al. (Stanford University Press, 1981), pp. 258–9.

2. Accounting for the narrative structure has been the impetus behind two recent, fine articles of *The Tenant of Wildfell Hall*: Jan Gordon, op. cit., and Naomi Jacobs, 'Gender and Layered Narrative in *Wuthering Heights* and *The Tenant of Wildfell Hall*', *The Journal of Narrative Technique*, 16, 3 (1986).

3. George Moore, op. cit., pp. 253–4, is the earliest and most emphatic voice on the subject of Anne Brontë's narrative infelicities. He is joined by other, later critics, notably Winifred Gérin, 'Introduction', *The Tenant of Wildfell Hall*, op. cit., p. 14.

4. Jan Gordon, op. cit., p. 722.

5. Charlotte Brontë, *Shirley*, op. cit., p. 323.

6. Jan Gordon, op. cit., p. 728.

7. Mary Wollstonecraft, *A Vindication of The Rights of Woman* (ed.) Carol Poston (New York, W. W. Norton, 1975), p. 63.

8. Ibid., p. 67.

9. George Moore, op. cit., p. 253.

## Notes to Chapter 6

1. Cited by Miriam Allott, 'Introduction', *Critical Heritage*, op. cit., p. 60.

2. Ibid., pp. 29–30.

3. 'Biographical Notice', op. cit., p. 6.

4. Ibid., p. 6.

5. Ibid., p. 8.

6. George Moore, op. cit., p. 253.

7. Miriam Allott, 'Introduction', op. cit., p. 46.

8. Will T. Hale, *Anne Brontë: Her Life and Writings* (Bloomington, Indiana University, 1929), p. 43.

9. Ibid., p. 44.

10. George Moore, op. cit., pp. 256–8.

11. Miriam Allott, 'Introduction', op cit., p. 49.

# Bibliography

## Selected Works by Anne Brontë

*Agnes Grey* (London: J. M. Dent, 1958).

*The Brontës: Their Lives, Friendships, and Correspondence* (eds)
T. J. Wise and J. A. Symington, 4 vols (Oxford, Shakespeare
Head, 1932).

*Poems* by Currer, Ellis and Acton Bell (London, Aylott and
Jones, 1846).

*The Poems of Anne Brontë: A New Text and Commentary* (ed.)
Edward Chitham (London, Macmillan, 1979).

*The Tenant of Wildfell Hall* (ed.) G. D. Hargreaves (Harmondsworth, Penguin, 1980).

## Selected Works about Anne Brontë

Allot, Miriam (ed.), *The Brontës: The Critical Heritage* (London,
Routledge and Kegan Paul, 1974).

Auerbach, Nina, *Woman and the Demon: The Life of a Victorian
Myth* (Cambridge, Harvard University Press, 1982).

Bell, Craig A., 'Anne Brontë: A Re-Appraisal', *Quarterly Review*
ccciv (1986), pp. 315–21.

Bentley, Phyllis, *The Brontë Sisters* (London, Longmans, Green
and Co., 1950).

Chitham, Edward and Tom Winnifrith, *Brontë Facts and Brontë
Problems* (London, Macmillan, 1983).

Christian, Mildred G., 'The Brontës' in *Victorian Fiction: A
Guide to Research* (ed.) Lionel Stevenson (Cambridge, Harvard
University Press, 1964).

Costello, Priscilla H., 'A New Reading of Anne Brontë's *Agnes
Grey*', *Brontë Society Transactions*, 19, 3 (1987), pp. 113–18.

Craik, W. A., *The Brontë Novels* (London, Methuen, 1968).

Duthie, Enid Lowry, *The Brontës and Nature* (New York, St Martin's Press, 1986).

Eagleton, Terry, *Myths of Power: A Marxist Study of the Brontës* (London, Macmillan, 1975).

Easson, Angus, 'Anne Brontë and the Glow-Worms', *Notes and Queries*, 26 (1979) pp. 299–300.

Ellmann, Mary, *Thinking About Women* (London, Macmillan, 1969).

Ewbank, Inga-Stina, '*The Tenant of Wildfell Hall* and *Women Beware Women*', *Notes and Queries*, x (1963), pp. 449–50.

Ewbank, Inga-Stina, *Their Proper Sphere: A Study of the Brontë Sisters as Early Victorian Female Novelists* (Cambridge, Harvard University Press, 1966).

Gaskell, Elizabeth, *The Life of Charlotte Brontë* (Harmondsworth, Penguin, 1975).

Gérin, Winifred, *Anne Brontë* (London, Allen Lane, 1959; rpt. 1976).

Gérin, Winifred, *Branwell Brontë* (London, Thomas Nelson, 1961).

Gilbert, Sandra M. and Susan Gubar, *The Madwoman in the Attic: The Woman Writer and the Nineteenth-Century Literary Imagination* (New Haven, Yale University Press, 1979).

Gilligan, Carol, *In a Different Voice* (Cambridge, Harvard University Press, 1982).

Gordon, Jan B., 'Gossip, Diary, Letter, Text: Anne Brontë's Narrative Tenant and the Problematic of the Gothic Sequel', *English Literary History*, 51, 4 (Winter, 1984), pp. 719–45.

Hale, Will T., *Anne Brontë: Her Life and Writings* (Bloomington, Arden Library, 1929: rpt. 1975).

Hargreaves, G. D., 'Incomplete Texts of *The Tenant of Wildfell Hall*', *Brontë Society Transactions*, 16, 2 (1972), pp. 113–18.

Harrison, Ada M. and Derek Stanford, *Anne Brontë, Her Life and Work* (New York, The John Day Company, 1959).

Heilbrun, Carolyn, *Towards a Recognition of Androgyny* (New York, Harper Colophon, 1974).

Helsinger, Elizabeth, Robin Sheets, and William Veeder (eds) *The Woman Question*, 3 vols. (London, Garland Publishing, 1983).

Jacobs, Naomi M., 'Gender and Layered Narrative in *Wuthering Heights* and *The Tenant of Wildfell Hall*', *The Journal of Narrative Technique*, 16, 3 (Autumn 1986), pp. 204–19.

McMaster, Juliet, '"Imbecile Laughter" and "Desperate Earnest" in *The Tenant of Wildfell Hall*', *Modern Language Quarterly*, 43, 4 (December 1982), pp. 542–68.

Moers, Ellen, *Literary Women* (New York, Doubleday, 1976).

Moore, George, *Conversations in Ebury Street* (New York, Boni and Liveright, 1924).

Ratchford, F. E., *The Brontës' Web of Childhood* (New York, Columbia University Press, 1941).

Rhodes, Phillip, 'A Medical Appraisal of the Brontës', *Brontë Society Transactions*, 16, 2 (1971), pp. 101–9.

Rosengarten, Herbert J., 'The Brontës' in *Victorian Fiction: A Second Guide to Research* (ed.) George H. Ford (New York: Modern Language Association of American, 1978).

Scott, P. J. M., *Anne Brontë: A New Critical Assessment* (New York, Barnes and Noble, 1983).

Showalter, Elaine, *A Literature of Their Own: British Women Novelists from Brontë to Lessing* (Princeton University Press, 1977).

Tiffany, Lewis K., 'Charlotte and Anne's Literary Reputation', *Brontë Society Transactions*, 16, 4 (1974), pp. 284–8.

Tillotson, Kathleen, *Novels of the 1840s* (Oxford University Press, 1956).

Vicinus, Martha (ed.), *A Widening Sphere: Changing Roles of Victorian Women* (Bloomington, Indiana University Press, 1977).

Winnifrith, Tom, *The Brontës and Their Background* (London, Macmillan, 1977).

Woolf, Virginia, *Death of the Moth and Other Essays* (New York, Harcourt Brace Jovanovich, 1942).

Woolf, Virginia, *A Room of One's Own* (Harmondsworth, Penguin, 1974).

# Index